*Red & Laretta,
accept this li
reminder of ho...
treasured "your friendship". May it
bring you some joy, some laughter
and maybe even a tear or two.*

A Life Packed Full

*Thanks for being true friends.
I still treasure your friendship
and covet your prayers.
Lovie*

EXCITING STORIES

A Life Packed Full

Dr. Frankie O. Phillips

TATE PUBLISHING
AND ENTERPRISES, LLC

A Life Packed Full
Copyright © 2014 by Dr. Frankie O. Phillips. All rights reserved.

No part of this publication may be reproduced, stored in a retrieval system or transmitted in any way by any means, electronic, mechanical, photocopy, recording or otherwise without the prior permission of the author except as provided by USA copyright law.

The opinions expressed by the author are not necessarily those of Tate Publishing, LLC.

Published by Tate Publishing & Enterprises, LLC
127 E. Trade Center Terrace | Mustang, Oklahoma 73064 USA
1.888.361.9473 | www.tatepublishing.com

Tate Publishing is committed to excellence in the publishing industry. The company reflects the philosophy established by the founders, based on Psalm 68:11,
"The Lord gave the word and great was the company of those who published it."

Book design copyright © 2014 by Tate Publishing, LLC. All rights reserved.
Cover design by Junriel Boquecosa
Interior design by Jimmy Sevilleno

Published in the United States of America

ISBN: 978-1-63185-298-5
Religion / Sermons / Christian
14.05.12

This book is dedicated to Lovie Phillips, who for over sixty years was the wife and partner of Syvelle Phillips. Together, they traveled as evangelists, pastored churches, and founded two ministries that touched lives around the world.

Acknowledgements

This book would not have been possible without the work done by my wife. Willette Phillips, over a period of several years, transcribed many sermons for Syvelle. At some point, she suggested to my brother that it would be a good idea to extract his stories from the sermons and perhaps put them into a collection. He liked the idea, but was too busy for another project. After his death, I was drafted by the Holy Spirit to undertake the task of compiling and editing selected stories to tell the larger story of how God used my brother to found and lead a global Bible translation ministry that has changed the lives of many people around the world, plus many who have been blessed by being a part by supporting the work.

Willette's work played a critical part in preserving Syvelle's sermons and stories. Without her work, something of great value would have been lost. She has been a great help to me as I have compiled and edited. All who benefit from this work should be grateful for the individuals who have played key roles. Two other ladies deserve special recognition: Lovie Phillips, Syvelle's wife; and Esther Barton, who worked with my brother from the early years of Evangel Bible Translators, and continues to serve the ministry.

Contents

Foreword 11
Introduction 13
The Preacher's Heart 15
The Young Preacher 25
The Evangelist and Pastor 35
Preaching 42
Partners in Ministry 51
The Book that Changed Everything 54
The Transition 62
The Early Years of Bible Translation 68
Translators 84
Missionaries and Translators 97
Adventures 114
The White Coat 118
True Dedication 122
Going to Goeno 126

The Holy Spirit Works	141
God's Mysterious Ways	147
Genius of the Holy Spirit	160
The Holy Spirit is a genius!	163
People and Places	165
God Doesn't Give Up	183
Outguessing God	195
New Dimensions of Ministry	204
The Lady Who Could Have Run the Red Cross	208
Miscellaneous Stories	217
Condensed Messages	233
Conclusion	259

Foreword

I had the good fortune of meeting Syvelle Phillips in the summer of 1950 when he came to preach a revival at our little church in Sayreton, Alabama. My good fortune turned into a relationship that marked both our lives, and influenced ministry to many people at home and abroad. After the first church service, I met with him and during that session I told him that I was struggling with the "call to preach" and needed some serious advice. I will never forget my first question to this twenty-one-year-old evangelist, "Syvelle, how do you preach?" On that day a sixty-two-year long relationship began. For these decades we have been "brothers." We have worked together in our ministries and we have been devoted friends.

Without doubt, Syvelle Phillips was one of the great preachers of the twentieth century. He was not only effective preaching to the masses throughout the world, but was a highly experienced and qualified communicator to preachers in remote areas around the world. He was correctly called "The Preacher's Preacher," and it is impossible to calculate the results of his God-given communication abilities. He was truly anointed and lead by the Holy Spirit. He encouraged and inspired thousands of other preachers.

He reached millions of people around the world, and he was truly a world-renowned preacher. I encourage you to read this book carefully. Some of the stories in Syvelle's sermons throughout more than sixty years of preaching will make you cry, some will make you shout for joy, but all of them will be a tremendous blessing, and will undoubtedly help you feel the richness of the spiritual experiences about which he spoke. Not only have countless numbers of souls been saved through the sermons that he preached around the world, but marriages have been reunited, homes restored, lives changed, many called to serve, and many led to a deeper experience with Jesus Christ. Yes, there have been thousands, and maybe millions, reached through his preaching ministry, "the spoken word." With that in mind I would be in error not to mention the tremendous impact of Evangel Bible Translators, "the printed word." Under Syvelle's leadership, this ministry has reached millions of people who would never have had the Bible in their own language. While "the spoken word" has been silenced by his passing, "the printed word" can never be silenced! Only heaven will reveal the final count.

—Bob Smith,
Retired Pastor, Founder and President, PrecisionHusky
Hoover, Alabama, September 17, 2013

Introduction

This is a collection of thrilling stories that will make you laugh and cry, and will probably make you praise the Lord for His wonderful work. Syvelle Phillips told these stories in sermons preached over many years. Some of these stories would make exciting movies. While editing the stories, just enough commentary was added to keep the reader aware of time and space, and to give some orientation to make the stories tell the big story of how God used a tall, skinny boy from East Brewton, Alabama, who did not finish high school, to found and lead a global Bible translation ministry that has touched the lives of thousands around the world.

As a result of his ministry, hundreds of thousands now have the Word in their own language. Many have reported that millions heard him preach over a period of more than sixty years, and many said that he was the "best preacher they'd ever heard." H. Syvelle Phillips was truly a world-renowned preacher. He preached in almost every state in the US. He preached in Canada and around the world in France, Russia, China, India, Nepal, Nagaland, Ghana, Liberia, Peru, Guatemala and other South American countries, Mexico, Sri Lanka, Fiji, several Pacific Islands, Malaysia, Benin, Philippines, New Guinea, and others. Selected sermon material, edited by Syvelle's brother, Dr. Frankie O. Phillips, was added to enhance the flavor of the big story, and give perspective to a life packed full. Scripture quotations are from the Authorized Version of the King James Bible, unless otherwise noted.

The Preacher's Heart

Editor's note:

Before you read the stories that make up the main part of this book, you need to know the heart of the preacher who told the stories. As you read, try to hear the voice and hear the heart of a man of God who dedicated his life to giving the Word to others. This message to a group of preachers sums it up. Listen to the Preacher.

I **was speaking to** a ministers' conference outside the US, when a group of young ministers came to me and said, "We have a request to make. We want you to stop preaching and tell us the story of your longevity in the ministry, and in your marriage." They continued, "We know about the disasters in ministries in America. The news reaches us out here. We have our own disasters, but we do not want to fail God. We want to be in this work for the long haul, so if there is anything you can share with us that would help, we would rather hear that than another sermon."

Let me tell you about the audience to which I was preaching. Early on, I had felt the importance of getting acquainted with the people and learning something about them. These fellows were from Singapore, Malaysia, Indonesia, and the Philippines—the Pacific basin. On one occasion, to help me get to know them, I asked some questions: "How many of you are first generation Christians—the first member of your family to know Christ as your personal Savior?" Over ninety percent of the hands were raised. Then I asked, "How many of you were Buddhist?" About one-third of the hands were raised. "How many of you were Hindu?" Another third of the hands were raised. "How many of you were Muslims?" Another third raised their hands. I then asked, "How many of you have been saved less than ten years?" Almost all of them indicated that they had been saved less than ten years.

I was speaking to a gathering of over two hundred young ministers, some of whom were leading churches of over one thousand members. These men were pastors of significant churches, and had not been saved more than ten years. They were obviously very sharp. What a challenge and what a privilege to speak into their young lives. When they came to me with the request to stop preaching, and tell them how my wife and I had maintained our marriage, and had maintained our enthusiasm in the joy of the Lord and for the ministry, I was really shocked. I had never thought of that. I had never entertained the idea that there was a formula or a track to run on. Somehow we had just done it. We were survivors—victorious survivors, and I did not have a clue as to how to answer them.

I went back to the hotel that night shaken in my soul. My first thought was, *How did I do that?* I knew, of course, that it was the grace and mercy of God. That goes without saying. I knew that it was not because of genius on our part. I knew that we were nobodies from nowhere, and had never thought in terms of some kind of philosophy to embrace, or formula that we could work out. We were just saved by grace, and we were chugging along trying to keep our sanity, trying to stay saved and to stay married, while surviving the rigors of a Pentecostal ministry.

I was really dogged by their questions. I began to realize that people who had been married forty-five to fifty years (it was then fifty-one for us), and had been in the ministry that long were few. We have been blessed. Some of you are right there with us, and others of you are not far behind. How do you survive and maintain a sense of victory, joy, and enthusiasm? What keeps you from being a cynic? What keeps you from falling into sin? What keeps you moving ahead in the ministry? Those questions really troubled me that night, because I had never been forced to think about them.

As the night went on, I slept very little as I wrestled with these questions. I began to realize that at crisis points in our lives, God had made truth real to us, truth that sustained us. I began to realize that it was not an emotional experience that sustained us; it was truth. It goes without saying that you begin at the beginning. You must know that you were really born again. I have always had an incredible sense of call. Since I was a little boy, I knew I was born to preach. I have never doubted the call. I think it is okay to take out your call every now and then and look it in the face, but to perpetually wonder if you are called to preach has to be a miserable way to live. You ought to know that you know that you know that you are born again; that you have a divinely assigned destiny; that God has given you a purpose, he set you apart; and, God in his sovereign grace, and in spite of all your weaknesses and frailties, chose to partner with you in making you a blessing to the world. Question marks ought not to linger over the call of God.

Then I began to be able to mark junctures and crossroads in my life, crises, times when I needed fresh revelation from God, remembering that again and again the Holy Spirit was faithful to give me the truth I needed to take one more step forward. I have never been able to draw strength from an emotional experience. I have drawn strength from truth. That is why I still wonder at the value that is being placed on physical manifestation today. I know there can be a physical response to the supernatural, but I do not believe that you can put a premium on your ministry by how many people fall flat. If God blesses you that way, fine, but do not try your stuff on me, because I am not going to give you a courtesy drop. If it is truly God, I'm okay with it.

I was able to identify over thirty junctures where God came through and gave me the strength and understanding I needed to get beyond another crossroad and another crisis. The way God worked with me that night was to take me down memory lane and let me relive the junctures, the crossroads, the crises, the times when he came and revealed a nugget of truth that I was able to lay hold of and let it minister to me. If Lovie and I have any testimony, it is that we are survivors; we are victorious survivors. I tell you that in God's name he will give you strength for the journey, and he will help you to finish strong! Let us praise God for the cleansing stream, the sanctifying work of the Holy Spirit. It takes out the bitterness. It takes out the disappointment. It takes out the pain and resentment and leaves us clean and fresh. Abide in the vine and stay connected to the river. (There are stories in the next chapter about the vine and the river.)

There is power in making an irrevocable commitment. The idea of leaving the ministry, the idea of not serving God is totally foreign to me. I made a commitment. I do not believe in eternal security in the extreme sense that some of our friends do, neither do I believe in backsliding in the sense that many others do. You will get what you preach. If you preach backsliding, you will have a crop of it. I believe that we are very secure. I believe that it is very hard to get away from the grace of God. I believe that it is difficult for you to resign. I believe it is difficult for you to get out of the ministry. I believe that God will pursue you and be merciful to you. I believe that God will even let you talk foolishly, and not pay any attention to what you say. But, if you are bound and determined to go to hell, I think he will let you. If you are bound and determined to leave the ministry, I suppose that he really does not need draftees. But for me, a long time ago I bound myself to the altar with cords that cannot be broken; and God entered into a covenant, that if I would furnish the man he would furnish the grace. He has been great at furnishing grace.

I have made it a habit down through the years to every now and then have a real personal session with God, and I say, "God, I did not come today to ask you for anything. This is a blessed season, and I have peace and quiet in my spirit. I am not fighting any big battles. As far as I know my mind is clear and my heart is clean. While I am thinking straight, I want to tell you that I love you, and I want to tell you that I love the idea of being a preacher. I thank you for calling me, and I thank you for the ministry you have given me, and I thank you for the privilege of serving you. God, while I am thinking clearly and under no pressure, I want to tell you that this prayer supersedes any prayer that I might pray tomorrow. If I come back tomorrow and have foolish things to say, be gracious and ignore me. This is the prayer that counts."

As long as you tinker with the thought of giving up the ministry, as long as you tinker with the thought of getting a divorce, or leaving your church, the devil will use that to pry you loose from your commitment. Cords that cannot be broken bind the sacrifice that I put on the altar a long time ago. If God is willing to put up with me, I am committed to him, and his grace is sufficient.

Another great truth that God made real to me so many years ago along this line is that he is not a hard taskmaster. I have discovered that his yoke is easy and his burden light. I simply cannot understand preachers who spend hours and hours wallowing in their own misery, talking about what a dirty deal they got when God called them to preach. I have no time for people who gave up a career in show business to be a preacher. The highest honor that God could ever give a human being is to be a spokesman for the living Savior, and there is no place in the ministry for self-pity. Sure we get tracks on our backs. There is a price to pay. Sure there are unpleasant things we have to deal with; but, I would dare say that without exception every man and woman who is in the ministry is wearing better clothes, eating better food, driving a better car, and living in a better house than you would be if you were not on God's payroll. You might not make as much money, but God has a way of adding to and blessing you and multiplying you; and I will guarantee you that your health is better. The ministry is not a robber; it is a blessing. Celebrate the privilege! I believe that God wants to reveal himself to us at every juncture. I am not encouraging you to look for some spectacular vision or some phenomenal physical experience. That may come, and if so, enjoy it and celebrate it, but God has a way of intercepting you at the point of your need, and he has a way of giving you just the strength you need to keep going. Understand that God is not a difficult taskmaster. You are partners with him, and he knows your weaknesses and frailties. He knows that you are human.

I heard about one of these super prophets, and I decided that I would go and see what was going on. I went to this hotel ballroom with about five or six hundred people. This fellow did not seem to be doing anything wrong. Basically, he was giving everybody a scripture and saying, "This is the scripture God brings to mind for you. You can bank on it." He was taking them one at a time and going along pretty well. I was trying to be tolerant and patient with all of this, thinking that there could not be anything wrong with giving someone a verse.

About an hour into the service he got tired (he was an older man). Suddenly, he said, "Folks, I am exhausted and cannot prophesy over any more of you one at a time so I am going to prophesy pew by pew." He did a grand gesture and said, "That pew back there, everybody on that pew is going to get a new car."

They latched onto that in a hurry. He did another grand gesture and everybody on the next pew was going to get a new house. He said, "You have been praying for a new house, and God is going to give you a new house." By now he was to my pew. He made his grand gesture and said, "Everybody back there on that pew is going to get a new baby at your house. You have been praying for a baby, and God is going to give you one." When he said that, a woman sitting on the end of the pew jumped up and said, "Not me, brother, I am out of here!" She and her friend went out the door, and I was right behind them. Then people wonder why we have doubts about this kind of ministry.

I am saying that we have to learn that we are frail; yes, we are weak; yes, we have shortcomings; yes, we are human, but God understands. He does not demand perfection from those who would speak in his name. There is mercy and grace for the man of God (Hebrews 4:16). There is elbow room to be human and to move and do the best you can. God will forgive you when you make mistakes. God will compensate for your weakness. He is your partner. He is your God. The *truth* that God ministers to you is the thing that will sustain you. You do not get it all in one experience, or at one juncture of your life. As you need it, grace comes, and with it truth (John 1:14). As you need it, your understanding is enlarged. As you need it, God gives you understanding. As you need it, God shows you the way through the wilderness.

A person in my church gave me some tapes by a lady whose name I do not remember. She was very articulate. She told how she lived so close to God that in the mornings when she dressed, she stood in her closet and prayed asking God which dress she should wear and she said that the Holy Spirit gave her directions as to which clothes she should wear. For a reason I cannot explain, I began to think how wonderful that someone could live so close to God.

One morning I was standing in my closet looking at this rack of old suits, and I remembered the sweet teaching of that lady. I said, "God, if it makes any difference to you what I wear today, please speak to me and tell me which suit to wear, and I will be pleased to wear it."

Suddenly I heard like thunder in my soul, "I am not your mother!" I was startled and turned to see who had spoken. Again this voice came, "I am not your mother. I am your father. Fathers do not care what their boys wear. Just get your clothes on, get out of here, and go to work."

I learned from that experience that God is not my mother, and that he gives me a lot of latitude in the decisions I make. The farther I walk with God the more faith he has in me and the more faith I have in him. Just as my faith grows in him, his faith in me grows, and I do not need nearly as much personal prophecy as I did when I was thirteen years old. If I do make a mistake, he is merciful. God is not your mother, so get out of here and go to work!

As I look back across years of ministry, I can tell you that *truth* saves. On one occasion, I was healed of ulcers while working in a youth camp. I went to the camp kitchen, drank the remainder of the goat's milk, threw away the baby food, and in three days I was completely well. Truth healed me! I got my thinking straightened out. I learned that I am totally and absolutely dependent upon God. I preach almost every day of my life now, but I never approach the pulpit feeling like I know what to do or how to do it. I always have the feeling that I had back there as a teenaged boy, a feeling of helplessness and of not knowing what to do, but having the assurance that all I have to do is stay connected to the vine. If I stay connected, the juice flows. You do not have to make your church grow. You do not have to make people do anything. You just abide in the vine and let the sap flow. The fruit will come!

I believe with all my heart that I can say that Lovie and I are not bitter, old people. If I know my heart, we are not cynical, and we are not bitter. We have had garbage dumped on us. All kinds of people have brought garbage and tried to dump it in our spring. It was not our righteousness or our genius or our theological understanding, but it was our connection not only to the vine but also to the river. When we give opening for that river to flow it pushes out all the debris. There is no place for garbage, no place for bitterness, no place for doubt. It is pushed aside by the flow of the Holy Spirit. If there is a lot of garbage in your life clogging up the spring, you should ask God to open the valve and turn on the pressure. Rules and regulations will never clean the spring. Doctrine and creed will never clean it, but if you will plug into the river, out of and through your innermost being will flow spiritual strength and spiritual power, and it will not matter what is dumped on you. When it is all over, the spring will still be clean, and the river will still be flowing, and you will not be the depository for garbage.

Any man or woman who fully accepts the call to proclaim the gospel of Jesus Christ enters a spiritual war zone, and is subject to attack. You can expect it, and you must be prepared for it. Don't be surprised if its source comes from something that bears the label of religion, even Christian. In this world today, religion is the greatest enemy of the gospel. It was that way in the time that Jesus lived; and it got him killed. So you are not exempt. I could tell you a hundred stories, but I will only tell you two short ones.

Years ago, a friend of mine who was a neighboring pastor, shared with me a very powerful and private experience: One day the deputy sheriff of the county came to his house and said to him, "Reverend, because I am your friend I am going to tell you something that I think you ought to know. There is a preacher in this town telling that you are a practicing homosexual."

My friend said that to his utter amazement and for the first time in his life, a wave of absolute hatred swept over him, and he had the urge to kill. He said, "I was so shocked when I realized that I could react with murder in my heart. I jumped in my car and drove to a secluded area on the beach. I climbed over the sand dunes and got down in a ravine where I knew I would have privacy, and threw myself on the ground in the sand. I said to God in agony of soul, 'there is something deeply wrong with me that would make me feel such hot hatred for a man, and I will not leave here until you cleanse me of that hatred and remove the desire to kill from my heart.'"

He interceded on behalf of himself and on behalf of his accuser until the agony was over and a release of the spirit took place, and the joy of the Lord was his again. He got back in his car and drove back to town. He said, "And as God would have it, the first person I saw was that man. I got out of my car and walked over to him, put my arm around his shoulder, and said, 'My brother, I have no idea what would make you tell such a horrible thing, but I want you to know that earlier today, if I had seen you I would have killed you, but I feel nothing but love and pity for you, and it is only because of the grace of God."

Another preacher friend, who had become a successful evangelist, made a decision which brought a flood of criticism. When his father, who was the county sheriff in a west Florida county, suddenly died, the county officials asked my preacher friend to accept the office of sheriff to replace his father. He accepted, and therefore had little time for evangelistic work as he had been doing it. He faced much criticism from fellow Christians and his denomination. When he told me the story, he was still hurting. He told me that in the position of sheriff he could witness to many more people than he could preaching revivals. He went on to be a strong witness in his role as sheriff, and was invited to speak to groups that he would never have been able to witness to otherwise. Later, he was able to serve as a Florida State Senator. He remained a strong Christian witness.

The Young Preacher

Editor's note:

These stories that he told in sermons over several decades reflect God's mercy and grace in accomplishing his destiny in a life. My brother's life demonstrated the acts of the Holy Spirit in a miraculous way. He lived a life packed full of miracles. It started in the summer of 1941, while we were living in Mobile so our daddy could work in the shipyard. Some unknown evangelist put up a tent two blocks from our little house. One night, my brother and I walked down the sawdust aisle to kneel at a plank that served as an altar. A few weeks later, I turned seven and he turned twelve. When we get to Heaven, we will find that man whose effort and sacrifice put that tent there to preach the gospel in our neighborhood.

The Calling

When I said yes to God for the ministry, I was eighteen years old. My daddy owned some old trucks that hauled logs. He was having a hard time keeping a driver on one of these trucks, and I said to my dad, "I can drive that truck."

He said, "You are too light weight. You are just a skinny kid."

"Dad, I have worked around these trucks as long as you have had them, and I can drive that thing."

He got me a hard hat, and I got in that monster and drove it. On this one trip, the trailer was loaded with thirty full-length trees that the bark had been peeled from. These trees would later be treated with creosote and used to make utility poles. With the bark off the trees they were as slick as if they had been lubricated.

I was coming down a long grade with this monstrous load behind me, heading for a rickety wooden river bridge. I had to negotiate a turn, and while doing so the steering wheel became loose in my hands and made a full turn. It had lost contact with the front wheels, because the steering gear had come completely apart, and I had no control over the rig. The brakes were already smoking. There was a forty-year-old man riding in the truck with me, and he panicked. I had to tell him to jump for his life, but he was so frightened that he could not find the door handle. He was screaming while I was trying to shift all the gears and work with the emergency brake. The truck was completely out of control. I reached across the man, opened the door and practically pushed him out.

As he went out the door, he begged me to jump, but I thought of the money my daddy had in that rig, and I said, "Oh God, just one more time, let me stop this thing." That truck stopped within eighteen inches of the riverbank. If the tires had made one more revolution the truck would have dropped perhaps thirty feet down to the river.

I could not open the door on the driver's side because there was a tree limb across the windshield and against the door. I had to get out on the right hand side of the truck. When it was all over, and I saw how close I had come to being killed, the Lord said to me, "I have a great work for you to do. I have called you. The devil tried to kill you to keep you from doing what I have called you to do."

Since that day I have traveled in the merciful arms of a protecting God. "For he shall give his angels charge over thee to keep thee" (Psalms 91:11).

I started preaching when I was eighteen years old. My pastor recognized the call of God on my life, and it shocked me when he put his arm around my shoulders and asked me when I was going to start preaching. I could hardly answer him. How could he know that God had called me? I had never talked to him or anyone else about it. My mother always thought my brother was going to be the preacher, so I had not discussed my call with her. I stood there looking at him in astonishment, and he said, "I think you had better preach Wednesday night. We might as well get you started."

That Wednesday night my car bogged down in a mud puddle, and I was an hour late getting to church. When I finally got to church, I had mud on my shoes and was a mess. Sitting there was my old uncle who had been preaching for fifty years—a crusty, old hell-fire-and-damnation preacher that scared the wits out of everybody. I thought, *Oh, praise God, Uncle Dan has been asked to preach!*

Without looking around, he got out of his seat, walked all the way to where I was sitting and said, "I see the preacher has gotten here," and he handed me his Bible. I was scared within an inch of my life. My knees were literally knocking together.

I went to the pulpit, read my text, and began. About two minutes into my sermon, the Spirit of God came upon me—from the top of my head to the soles of my feet. It felt like warm oil, and it was electric! I'm sure you other preachers know how it felt. I tasted the anointing for the first time. That is a delicious taste.

The anointing is addictive, and if you ever plug into it once, nothing else will ever satisfy. I do not know what I said (there were no tape recorders in those days), but my mother and her entourage of Pentecostal sisters were out in the aisle dancing.

I have no idea how I closed the sermon or how I stopped, but the word was out that the Phillips boy was preaching. By the next Sunday, I had another invitation and then another one. I was off and running, but I don't know how. I prayed for the sick and they were healed. I gave altar calls and people ran to the altar. I just didn't know any better than to believe God; and he responded mightily.

I came from a poor family and there was no hope of going to Bible School. I was trying to preach and work on a job at the same time. My daddy, who was not saved at that time, gave me some good advice. He said, "Son, if God called you to preach, I think you ought to go preach. If he has called you to work, you should work. You are killing yourself trying to do both. I have no money to give you, but you always have a home to come to." His assurance that he thought I was called to preach was the encouragement that I needed.

Two years before my daddy died, I had the privilege of leading him in that prayer that he had put off for so long. When we meet in Heaven, he will be an equal member in the family of God. Finally, I decided against going to Bible School. I acquired many good books and proceeded to educate myself. I completed the Berean Correspondence School of the Bible offered by the Assemblies of God and was ordained at the age of twenty.

I opened a little church that had been abandoned, cleaned out the dust, turned on the lights, and announced that we were going to have a revival meeting. The church filled up and the yard filled up. I did not have enough people to help me pray. There were only about seven saved people in the building. At the close of the service about twenty people came to the altar. Those were exciting times. I was on my way!

Churches everywhere wanted me to come and preach. I did not know how to dress or much about anything. I did know that God's hand was upon me, and it was an exciting and glorious launch. Hundreds of people were saved and miracles of healing took place. A cancer slid off a lady's face. A blind girl started screaming during a service, "I can see!" I had never seen anything like that, but God was using me. I was just a boy.

Then, a dry season came. I reached a place where I could not pay anyone to come to the altar. I held three revival meetings and not one soul was saved. I could not beg anyone to get excited about me or what I was preaching. It was a desert experience, and I began to wonder if I had sinned against the Holy Spirit, or committed some other sin. I had no one to talk to. My pastor did not know much more about preaching than I did. As I wondered what was happening, the devil came and began to make accusations against me. I had not experienced this kind of attack. I was in a new arena. I had gotten intoxicated with sudden success, and here I was in the desert. I began to wonder if my preaching career had come to a close. I took this situation so seriously and personally that it caused me to develop ulcers. I was put on a diet of goat's milk and baby food. I was nineteen years old, skin and bones, and feeling that something was wrong with me because God was withholding his blessings.

Abide in the Vine

About that time, I was invited to come to north Alabama to help with a youth camp. I discovered Christian books. An old man did me a great favor by giving me a brown paper bag full of paperback books. He said, "Son, if you will read these, they will do you good." They did me more good than I could ever have imagined. Among those books was one by F. B. Meyer. I climbed up the mountain side, put my feet in a stump hole that was filled with brown leaves, pulled out the book by F. B. Meyer, and read his classic sermon based on the passage of scripture about the importance of abiding in the vine.

I began to read that great message in which he made the point that the branch cannot produce fruit on its own, but is totally dependent upon the vine. The sap, the juice, and the nutrients flow up through the vine and into the branches, and this is the process that produces fruit. The branch has nothing to do with producing fruit, except to abide. When I finished reading that message I knew what was wrong. I had been trying too hard in my own strength. God loved me enough that he had cut off that flow in order to position me to learn a valuable truth that has affected my life until this day. How amazing that a sermon preached years ago and later printed was put into a brown paper bag and handed to a novice young preacher to change his life forever—and to some extent change thousands of lives. That is grace and truth, and the work of the Holy Spirit. The Holy Spirit did not quit at the end of the Book of Acts.

Editor's note:

> This story so vividly makes the point of the importance of the printed word. The publishers of those little books were part of the great story that started in the book of Acts and continued through my brother's life.

In fact, by that passage of scripture in my Bible I have written a note that says, "Life changing!" In that moment when God quickened truth to me, my life was changed forever. I learned that I could not make things happen in the spiritual realm. I learned that I was not intelligent enough or strong enough to make supernatural things happen in my natural strength. What a lesson and what a contribution this revelation made to my longevity in the ministry. That was not the last desert I went through. I have been through others. I have been through seasons when there were no stars or moon, and the storm raged, but I never forgot that Syvelle Phillips could do nothing but abide. If you abide, the sap will flow and eventually the fruit will be produced.

"Abide in me and I in you. As the branch cannot bear fruit of itself, except it abide in the vine; no more can ye except ye abide in me. I am the vine, ye are the branches: He that abideth in me, and I in him the same bringeth forth much fruit: for without me ye can do nothing" (John 15:4–5).

I can tell you that *truth* saves. I was healed of ulcers. Truth healed me! I got my thinking straightened out. I learned that I am totally and absolutely dependent upon God. If I stay connected, the juice flows. You do not have to make your church grow. You do not have to make people do anything. You just abide in the vine and let the sap flow. The fruit will come!

When I started preaching, I was as tall as I am now and weighed 130 pounds. I weigh more than 200 this morning, so you can imagine about how skinny I was. My wife's description of me back then was anything but complimentary. I came to her church after she had just been saved. She received the Holy Spirit under my ministry (and she has needed it ever since). She said that the first time she saw me I was as skinny as a rail, and my ears were so big that I looked like a two-door car coming down the street with both doors open. All the church ladies had prayer for me because they thought I was dying of tuberculosis. Maybe I was, I do not know, but I was a pitiful sight to behold.

The River Flows

Lovie and I were newlyweds and we were preaching as evangelists in a country church down in south Alabama. The pastor said, "A group of preachers are going to meet over in the edge of

Florida for a picnic and fellowship time. Would you like to come with us?" Of course, we wanted to go, and we did.

We arrived early at the picnic site, which was near a small crystal-clear lake. While we were waiting for the other ministers to arrive, I wandered off down by the lake's edge. It is amazing what God uses to mold your life. It always comes in an unexpected way. I noticed that the water was crystal clear. There is a phenomenon in Florida of underground rivers that flow under the limestone formations. Rivers and streams flow out of sight and unseen, and then suddenly break through the crust of the earth and flow on the surface. Silver Springs is the most notable example of this. Florida is honeycombed with these limestone formations. This little lake was a small version of Silver Springs. I began to observe that out about one hundred feet from the shore was a boiling spring. Thousands of gallons of water were springing up and making the white sand boil. I had seen this type of thing before, but I observed that day that careless picnickers and fishermen had thrown beer cans, old rubber boots, broken fishing poles, picnic debris, and other rubbish into that body of water.

Where the spring was boiling up, there was no debris. The force of that underground river was clearing it away. As I stood there watching that phenomenon, suddenly into my mind came the scripture, "He that believeth on me...out of his belly shall flow rivers of living water" (John 7:38). I began to understand that there is more to being baptized in the Holy Spirit than just speaking in tongues, quivering, shaking, jerking, running, dancing, and getting excited. When you connect with that river of living water, and that river flows out of you and through you, it pushes all the junk and all the debris out of your life. It refuses to accept the garbage that people try to throw in to clog and stop the flow. The cleansing comes from the flow.

In those early years in rural areas where there were no churches, thousands gathered outdoors to hear the gospel. Hundreds were saved. Many were called into ministry. The trickle became a mighty stream that flowed across America and around the world. That was certainly much better than that river the devil tried to put me in when I was eighteen.

Drafted

I was preaching a revival when a delegation from the big church in Panama City, Florida, came to the meeting to audition me. (It was the largest Assemblies of God church in the US.) I knew why they were there, and I really showed out that night. I preached hell fire and damnation. They decided to have me come and preach anyway. I went down to look at the church. I had never been to a church that large. On my tour of the building, I learned that it had ninety Sunday school rooms and an auditorium that seated over one thousand people. In those days that was a huge church.

I remember going back to my room, throwing myself across the bed and saying, "God, if I strike out here, it is your fault. I did not ask to come here. I have never seen a church this size. I do not know how to act. There is no telling what I look like." (Before I got married I did not know that certain colored socks went with certain colored ties. I just thought they were clothes and you wore them.)

I remember sitting on the platform during the preliminaries. The guitars were out of tune, and everybody's nephew and niece had to sing. The church was packed, and I could hardly breathe. I never heard so much commotion, and it went on and on. I was partly hidden on the platform, and people kept trying to see the evangelist. When the pastor finally introduced me, there I stood, six foot two, 130 pounds, and nineteen years old. An audible sigh went up from that audience, and I could feel it.

Later a fellow who was saved at the meeting told me that he thought, "My God, do we have to listen to that for two weeks?" I felt these vibes coming from the audience, and I thought as I got up out of my corner and approached the pulpit, *You don't think I can preach, but I am going to show you a thing or two.* I got plugged into a live wire that night. I could not preach more than twenty minutes, but at the end of twenty minutes hundreds of people were on their feet praising God and forty people were in the altar for salvation. The revival went nonstop for several weeks.

I was not being arrogant. If anybody there knew I was unworthy, I did. If anybody there knew I was unqualified to be in that pulpit, I did. But I also knew that God had called me, and God had promised to be with me, and that is the greatest discovery that you will make in all of your life. It is a great thing to be able to say, "He is my helper." Not because my grandmother called me, and not because my pastor decided that I was a bright boy, but because God has said, "I will never leave thee; I will never forsake thee." You can go in the name of the Lord with that assurance. And you can stay connected to the vine, and in the flow of the river.

The Evangelist and Pastor

I was an evangelist for many years. In the days before it was popular and possible for evangelists to stay in motels and hotels, I was preaching a revival, and staying with the pastor and his family in the parsonage. The dear lady, the pastor's wife, would pray five hours a day. I thought when I first arrived that she was the most spiritual woman I had ever met, and that the church was going to experience a great revival.

Before I left there, I discovered that she was not praying. She was hiding from that sink full of dirty dishes, and those five rowdy boys that stormed in and out of the house totally undisciplined and uncontrolled. She was feeding both her husband and the evangelist cornflakes three times a day. She would have done the Kingdom of God a lot more good if she had prayed thirty minutes, then washed dishes, done some ironing, and spanked boys for a while. When I finally saw through the charade, I was mad, but I learned a valuable lesson. At the beginning of our marriage, I told my wife that I wanted her to pray, but I also wanted her to cook.

When I preached at the General Council of the Assemblies of God in Des Moines, Iowa, I was thirty-six years old, and this was an awesome assignment. There were probably three thousand young Assemblies of God preachers, and only one every two years gets chosen. When I was invited to speak, I considered it a high honor and a tremendous obligation and responsibility. I went to the Civic Auditorium and sat in every section during that week and listened to every speaker. The day before I was to speak the next night, I went on the platform, walked back and forth across the platform to get the feel of the whole thing. I talked to the soundman. I wanted the place to be familiar when I got up to speak. I wanted to feel that I was in surroundings where I had been before.

We Get Tired

Recently, I received a letter from an evangelist friend of mine who is noted for his vivacious personality, boundless energy, and an untiring zeal to do the work of God. This long letter poured out an unusual confession from this man. I had never heard expressions from him such as, "I am so weary. My correspondence has become a drag to me. Even the preaching of God's Word has become an ordeal. The traveling is so demanding that I have felt that I could not go on."

As I read that letter, I remembered a period in my life when I felt that I just could not face another congregation, could not make another decision, could not wrestle with another problem, and could not carry another burden. I was mentally, physically, and spiritually exhausted. I remembered what a beautiful thing it was to have God come to me in love, in tender kindness, and restore my soul, taking me by the hand and gently leading me into a rest that is found only near the heart of God.

It is not the work that we do that kills us. It is not the number of pounds that we lift or the number of miles we walk or chores we do, it is the stress, the strain, and the agitation that takes their toll. It is a paradox that God has promised his people rest—rest for the soul, rest for the mind, and rest for the spirit. Yet, so many of God's people do not fully appropriate the provisions of the living God. It is a sad thing to see a Christian that has responded to the call of the Spirit, yet is enjoying nothing of the promises and provisions of God for rest for the soul and the mind. "Rest in the Lord, and wait patiently for him" (Psalm 37:7).

Becoming a Pastor

I want to share with you one of the nicest things God ever did for me. I was a young evangelist and had preached many revival meetings. I was considered successful, but when it came time for me to pastor, I took a very small church in a fishing village in Florida. It was a wonderful experience for me, because I had never conducted a funeral. I had never presided over Communion. I had never performed a wedding. I did not know how to do those things. About all I could do was preach an evangelistic message. I had very little problem shifting to pastoral pulpit preaching and teaching, but I was a rank amateur in the management of a church and many other church duties. It would have been a tremendous tragedy for me to have taken on the responsibility of a large church with so little knowledge of how to do it.

Some churches in big cities asked me to consider being their pastor, but I knew that for my sake and for the future of my ministry, it would be better for me to begin that phase of my life where I had the freedom and elbow room to grow. I knew that anything I did in that village was most likely to be an improvement over what had been done. I also knew that I was inexperienced and very weak in some areas. The five and a half years I was there, I did weddings and funerals and communion, and a lot of other things. When the day came that an old, sophisticated church in southern California asked me to come and be their pastor, I had some background on which I could approach that church, knowing that I did not have all the answers but at least I was not scared out of my wits.

Every service we have in this church (Santa Ana First Assembly) is different, and I believe that that is ordered of the Holy Spirit, because there is one reason for our having church and that is to see that human needs are met. I pray continually that God will tailor every service to meet the most demanding needs present in that service. I have no way of judging what those needs might be. If I did try to judge the need, I would still have no solution. Even if I thought I had some prescription to offer I would still be powerless, because I have no resource that is capable of meeting human needs.

Suppose while sitting in a doctor's office waiting to see the doctor, as most of us do at one time or another, the doctor rushed out of his office, opened the door and tried to give a blanket diagnosis and the same prescription to everyone in the waiting room. That would be absolute chaos. A man with a broken foot would have needs different from a lady with a migraine headache. The person who has diabetes or ulcers needs altogether different treatments from the one who has a kidney disease. So every person has to be dealt with personally and individually.

When I come to the pulpit as a pastor, I come to speak to all of you collectively, knowing that all of you have individual needs and knowing that unless there is a supernatural dimension, not only to what I say but also to what you hear; the preaching becomes an empty mockery. It amazes me every Sunday to learn what different people hear me say or what they understand that I said. That amazement is not consternation. In a way, it is verification of the Holy Spirit's unique work in the preaching of the Word of God. There is a sense in which the Holy Spirit is not only the author of the message, and the one who gives the unction and freedom to deliver the message, but there is also a sense in which he is the interpreter of the message. He is the one who makes application of the message.

I plead with you to pray with me for a supernatural dimension to what I have to say, not only in and around this pulpit but there where you sit. Between my lips and your soul I want the Holy Spirit to color, turn, and apply what I say until it becomes meat and drink for every one of you, no matter in what mood or attitude, or with what need you might have come to the house of God. To me, preaching the Word of God is a sacred and holy experience. It is not making a speech. It is not giving a lecture. I absolutely refuse to try to work from a script, because I believe there should be spontaneity, and I believe that a man of God should be free to sense in his spirit what God would have him say. If you really believe in the supernatural dimensions of preaching, you believe God can take his Word and make it apply to every person there in some special way. Do you believe that? Do you want that?

Let's go to prayer. "Dear God, I believe what I have just read. I believe it with all of my heart, and I have believed it for many years. I have watched the Holy Spirit work as frail men, ordinary men, often men of less than desirable abilities, would stand to speak in your name, daring to speak in your name as an exercise of faith and obedience to the call that was upon their lives. I have seen you through the spoken word communicate truth to the point that men and women left the service with changed hearts, changed attitudes, a new understanding of God, a new reason to live, and new courage to face tomorrow. That is exactly what I pray for today in Jesus's name. Amen."

Hippie Invasion on Sunday Morning

Dr. William Green, my dear friend and former associate pastor, was leading singing one Sunday morning when a group of hippies (probably fifty or sixty) invaded the church and tried to take over the service. Those woolly-looking characters (the first nucleus of the Children of God) had come to pronounce judgment on us. I am written up in their book, and if I act strangely, it is because they placed me "under a curse." They came into the church to take over.

When Dr. Green looked up and saw them coming down the aisle, he said, "My God, Syvelle, if you know anything to do, stand up and do it."

And, would you believe that even the deacons were willing for me to run the church that morning? They agreed unanimously for me to lead the way. I could see them out in the audience, and I knew they were thinking, "Go ahead!" But, the Lord had his way, and that is another story of how God can give a person supernatural power and supernatural authority to deal with people when there is a need.

We helped the "visitors" find seats, and I walked to the pulpit to read my text and begin the sermon. As I finished reading the text, the worst looking guy in the group, apparently the leader, leaped to his feet and yelled, "That is a damnable lie!"

I jumped off the platform and right into his face and said, "You sit down! What I have just read is the Word of God. It is not a damnable lie. You sit down!"

He dropped into his seat like I had shot him. Something supernatural was happening. God gave me authority—supernatural authority. I did not go back to the pulpit or look at my notes again. I preached the sermon, closed in prayer, and said to my people, "Get up; get your children and leave. I do not know what these people are about. I do not know who they are, but I know that they are up to no good. I would like for several of the men to remain with me until we can vacate the building. Please, the rest of you leave immediately."

The people, several hundred of them, were very cooperative. They slipped out of the church and quietly left. The hippies tried to interfere, but the people left as they were told.

The *Los Angeles Times* gave front-page coverage to the incident. The article read, "Six-foot-two Santa Ana pastor single handedly defies an army of hippies who try to take his pulpit." There was a big story and pictures. They said I put my finger on the nose of one of the hippies. I did not, but I came very close. When those fellows tried to take over my church, the Spirit of the Most High God came upon me with authority and boldness that I still cannot believe. It brought to mind, "Be strong in the Lord and in the power of his might" (Ephesians 6:10). They all stayed glued to their seats, and I preached my sermon, never missing a lick. The one that was making the most noise, I was on top of him.

As I walked across the parking lot later, I was shaken to the core. An older member of the church came to me, put his arm around my shoulders and said, "Son, you have been our preacher up until now. This morning you became our pastor." I had been pastoring the church only a few months.

Preaching

Back when I was a teenaged preacher, I got athlete's foot, and the Lord healed me. I prayed and he healed me. I put my feet back in those same shoes and got athlete's foot again, and God healed me again. After this was repeated about six times, I asked God what was going on. I said, "You heal me, and I break out with it again." The Lord said to me, "Burn all your socks. Get some new shoes." That was over fifty years ago, and I have not had another round of athlete's foot. Sometimes we need to burn our old socks. Sometimes we need to get rid of those infected shoes. It is far more God-honoring to make whatever is wrong right than it is to keep asking God for a rescue.

What the Lord really showed me and has continued to remind me of is that there are sources that create a load or an overload. One load (or overload) is created by "stuff." I not only collect stuff; I collect people. In the early days of our ministry I almost destroyed it because I got a dumb idea. I thought it was

Godly—a revelation from God. This is what I reasoned: "I know a lot of preachers who are 'on the shelf' discouraged and do not have anywhere to preach, and if I can find these fellows and bring them into the ministry, paying them a little 'get by' salary, I can minister to them every day and heal them while they help me get my work done." Dumb idea!

One day Lovie said to me, "One of the reasons I love you is because you have a tender heart, and I do not want you to ever lose that heart, but you have become an ambulance driver. You are out collecting all the broken people you can find. Do you think they are going to help you? They are killing us. They are going to destroy this ministry, because they are not getting well. They are eating at your expense, and they are destroying you. I want you to think and pray about getting rid of the whole crowd and starting over."

I hated to hear that. I could not believe that she was that "hard-hearted," but in that moment she had an understanding that I did not have. I was aggravated with her for several days about opposing what I was doing, but the longer I thought about it and prayed about it, the more sense it made. I had a housecleaning. They cried and carried on, but when it was all over, they were gone.

Another source of overload is people who want me to carry their load. A pastor knelt on the platform to pray, and two ladies came forward to kneel at the altar. They could see the soles of his shoes, and there were holes in them. One said to the other, "Look at our pastor's shoes. There are holes in the soles of his shoes. It is a shame for our pastor to be wearing shoes that have holes in the soles. I think we ought to buy him a new pair of shoes." The other lady said, "Honey, why don't you do it? You saw the need first."

One final point: One of the things that we need to lay aside (we are talking about unloading—laying aside every weight) is the weight that keeps us from running the race, not sin—weight. We need to know when to lay down some of the things that God has put on us, or we have put on ourselves. There are different kinds of seasons in your life; and there are seasons of responsibility, but when a season is over we need to recognize it. Sometimes it is hard to give up. We foolishly take ownership in things that God has already put aside.

I prayed down a million dollar piece of property and rejoiced over it. After a while I started thinking of it as my miracle. Nobody else prayed for it. I did, and God answered my prayer. There came a day when the miracle became a curse. We discovered that the building had asbestos in it. The roof leaked, and the cost to replace it would be $50,000. The septic system went out, which would cost another $50,000. Suddenly, my big miracle did not look so wonderful.

We did not need that property any more, and Lovie opened her mouth and dared to say, "Maybe we ought to think about selling it." I rebuked her, and said that I would thank her not to even mention it.

Later we were in a board meeting, and one of the board members dared to say out loud, "Maybe we ought to get rid of that group of buildings." It was a school of missions, and had served a wonderful purpose for a season. Being the chairman that I am, and in charge of everything, I rapped the gavel and moved on. How dare unbelief get into our ministry! The situation got worse.

I was up in Canada preaching at a ministers' conference, and I shared with those preachers how the ultimate punishment for the Romans was not to crucify a fellow but to take a dead body and strap it to his back and let the living walk around with the dead until death overcame the living. That was the ultimate torture. I was on a roll talking about how preachers take on dead things and how we need to let go of that which is dead. We had a great move of God. Preachers were crying and confessing that they were holding on to things that were dead. I was thinking, *My, I hit a home run today!* I was feeling real good about the sermon, and then I went home and dreamed—the only dream that I ever had that I really believe was from God.

I dreamed that this big, old house with fourteen bedrooms was on my back. I was struggling under its weight and about to be crushed. I dreamed that Jesus came out of the shrubbery with the biggest pair of scissors I had ever seen, and said to me, "If you will let me, I will cut the cords."

I said, "Please, Lord."

He cut the cords, and that big building rolled off my back and down the mountainside. I got up the next morning and said, "The battle is over. The Lord has given me release to let the old property go."

It took me two years to get rid of it, and if the guy I was selling it to had held out, I would have given it to him in another ninety days. All I got out of it was enough to recoup the deficit it had created. But, I was free! It had served a wonderful purpose for a season, and then the miracle became a source of death. Let God cut the cords. Do not hold on to that which has outlived its usefulness. Lay aside the weight and let God give you strength for the journey. "Let us lay aside every weight" (Hebrews 12:1).

While speaking at a ministers' conference in Ohio, I told the group that I am a preacher, and I love to preach. I fancy myself being prepared when I go to the pulpit. I put a high value on having something to say and knowing what to say and how to say it, and saying it in the name of the Lord. One night I was having a hard time. I had ten sermons I could have preached, but there was something about my integrity that said, "I am not willing to pull out number nineteen and preach it tonight. I need a fresh word from the Lord. I cannot bring myself to serve stale bread and pass out dull swords."

I was having a real struggle, which was unusual for me. I was sitting on the platform waiting to preach to perhaps four or five hundred preachers. I was trying desperately to figure out what the message for the night should be. Suddenly the Holy Spirit said to me, "Tell my people to renounce cynicism and bitterness and ask me to give them a tender heart."

Being the preacher that I am, I grabbed my Bible and looked for three verses. I quickly reached for my pen and began to write.

The Lord said, "Why don't you just do what I told you to do?"

"But, Lord, I can say all of that in thirty seconds."

"Why don't you just do what I told you to do?"

By now I am being introduced, and I do not have any options. I am on my feet walking to the pulpit. I said, "I do not understand what is going on. My style is to open the Bible, walk you through a passage of scripture and enjoy spreading a feast, but I do not have anything like that for you tonight. However, I will tell you what God just said to me, and I am going to leave the rest in his hands. The Lord instructed me to tell you to renounce cynicism and bitterness and a cold heart, and ask him to give you a tender heart." I repeated that three times, and following the third time, it was as if lightning struck the place.

Ministers who had probably never been slain in the Spirit found themselves flat of their backs on the floor. I am not into that kind of thing, but *bang!* Dozens of dignified pastors were on their hands and knees crawling to the altar—literally crawling. Talk about a meeting? We had one!

A cry went up from that gathering of preachers, "God, give me a tender heart! I reject bitterness and coldness of heart and cynicism, and I want a new tender heart." God answered that prayer and revolutionized perhaps hundreds of lives. That was all we did that night.

I believe that God would like for us to cry from our spirit, "God, flush out the bitterness. God, purge the cynicism. That thing that has been coming back to dog me and to make me angry and disappointed and frustrated—I release it and I want the flow to take that garbage downstream and out of sight so that I am fresh and alive in the things of God."

> **Editor's note:**
>
> Syvelle was on thirteen radio stations for twenty-five years on the west coast. The following is the introduction to one of his messages.

I pray that I can be a voice that God can use to speak directly to your heart. I often say that this ministry is not a game. It is not a joke. It is not something that I take lightly. It is serious ministry and I thank God for the anointing of the Holy Spirit that comes upon me when I come to this microphone. I am deeply grateful to God for the testimonies that pour into our office from people who are being blessed and whose lives are being changed because we dared put forth the effort to come to you day after day. If I did not believe that God answers prayer, if I did not believe that God is a miracle-working God who is able to meet every need, if I did not believe that God can express himself to us and reveal himself to us in such a way that we can receive the benefits of his love, I would despair and give up. But, I know that God is on the throne. I know that Jesus Christ lives today. I know that there is no man beyond the reach of God's love. There is hope and courage and strength available to any human being who will cry out to God. There is no dilemma that is too difficult for God, no situation too tangled, no life too battered and bruised that God cannot heal. God wants a chance to do something for you and to make his grace known in your life. "Now unto him that is able to do exceedingly abundantly above that we can ask or think according to the power that worketh in us" (Ephesians 3:20).

The Colonel Cusses

All of us know Colonel Sanders of Kentucky Fried Chicken. The old Colonel was eighty-plus years old and a multimillionaire, having sold his chicken franchise to the world. He was saved in an Assemblies of God church in Louisville, Kentucky. Sometime later, we were at an Assemblies of God convention. Of course, the whole fellowship was so proud that one of its churches had gotten this prized convert that they brought him to the convention to give his testimony.

With his beard and his white suit, he got up before ten thousand people and begins to testify about being born again, and right in the middle of his testimony he "cusses." He uses bad language! All the dignitaries—the "holy men of God"—were sitting on the platform ready to celebrate this prized convert, and there he was talking ugly. He was not just using slang words, he was cursing. He would testify about how wonderful it was to be saved, and in his exuberance he would use some choice words. Realizing what he was doing, the poor old fellow broke down and started crying. Weeping he said, "Folks, I am so sorry. I have used language that is not becoming to a Christian. I have been cussing since I was eight years old, and it is so much a part of my language that I cannot talk without those words coming out. I have embarrassed myself, and I am ashamed. Please forgive me, and please pray that I can get my vocabulary cleaned up."

The brothers were shocked. The sisters were in tears, but the whole crowd of us had to decide if we would flush him down the drain or open our hearts to him. Sometimes it takes a while for the Colonel to stop cussing. Sometimes it takes a while for a guy to stop smoking. Sometimes it takes a while to get a temper under control. Sometimes it takes a while to get a person completely delivered from drugs. Sometimes people limp their way into the Kingdom. I am absolutely convinced that there are not many victorious Christians in the whole world, but there are a lot of struggling pilgrims, and as long as the pilgrim is struggling but headed in the right direction, I want to walk with him and encourage him, because I, too, may be a struggling pilgrim.

You have to be patient and loving and never give up. I read about a pastor, who went to the bar and pulled a man out ninety-nine times before he got him sober and established in the church. As a pastor, I have worked with struggling people. I remember giving up on one family in a church in Florida. I said to Lovie, "You can go back to see them if you want to, but I am sick and tired of these people. I have put enough time and energy into them, and I am not going back. I am not trying any more. They are losers, and that is it! I am finished." Lovie would not give up on that family, and they became some of the strongest people in our church. "...for the Lord seeth not as man seeth; for man looketh on the outward appearance, but the Lord looketh on the heart" (Samuel 6:7).

If It's in the Book!

I heard Dr. Lloyd Olgivie speak at a pastor's seminar when he was the pastor of the prestigious North Hollywood Presbyterian Church. He told about how he was reading in the book of James when his attention was drawn to James 5:14–15, "Is any sick among you? Let him call for the elders of the church; and let them pray over him, anointing him with oil in the name of the Lord: And the prayer of faith shall save the sick." He said, "When I read that I stopped. I had never read those verses. I had completed seminary training, but I had never seen those verses The idea of anointing with oil and praying over the sick began to grip me. Finally I called my elders together and showed it to them. None of them had ever seen those verses either. So," he said, "we got into a big discussion about this scripture and what it meant, and finally we decided that if it is in the Book, we ought to do it. We announced an anointing service for a Sunday night. Now, nobody goes to Hollywood Presbyterian on Sunday night, but that Sunday night the church was filled. I had never anointed anybody and neither had the elders. All I knew to do was tell the congregation what had happened to me, and how this service came about. I just told them that I had discovered James 5:14–15, and had shared these verses with the elders of the church, and after much prayer and discussion we felt that since we are instructed in the Word to anoint we should do it. I asked members of the congregation who wanted to be prayed for to please come forward."

Being very dignified Presbyterians they had put silk pillows on the floor, one in front of each elder, which meant there were twenty-four silk pillows on the floor. Reverend Olgivie said that to their astonishment twenty-four people came forward. For the first time, a group of very shy and bewildered elders were faced with the responsibility of anointing and praying for these church members. Very timidly and shyly, they began the anointing service. God began to pour out his spirit. When those twenty-four had been ministered to they got up and twenty-four more came and twenty-four more, and twenty-four more, until hundreds of people had been anointed. And Dr. Olgivie said, "Brethren, it works! Try it!" He said, "You go home, and anoint the sick with oil, and pray the prayer of faith, and God will heal them!"

I was amazed to hear this sophisticated, highly educated, veteran pastor confirming a truth that my mother, Aunt Lena, Uncle Dan, sister Ruby, and sister Julia taught me when I was very young: *If it is in the Book, just do it.*

Partners in Ministry

Everybody in America knows the name Bill Gates and the name of his company, Microsoft. I was recently in the state of Washington, and a lot of the people out there in the churches work for the Microsoft Company. Some of them have gotten very rich partnering with him. A pastor friend of mine has one of Bill Gates's partners in his church.

One day he called up his pastor and said, "Pastor, I have good news. I just sent a ministry one million dollars."

The pastor told me, "The words were on the end of my tongue but somehow I sucked them back in, 'What do you mean you gave another ministry one million dollars, when we have a building program going here and you know that we want to get it completed? You are a member of this church, and your loyalty is here. What do you mean?' By the grace of God I did not utter those words."

There was silence on the phone, and the fellow on the other end asked, "Pastor, are you still there?"

He said, "When I had regained my composure enough that I could speak without resentment, I replied, 'Yes, I am still here.'"

The wealthy man said, "I want to tell you that for the next eighteen months I am going to be able to put a quarter of a million dollars a month into the building program of our church."

My friend said, "Talk about a close call. Talk about the mercy of God."

People in the state of Washington talk about when Bill Gates started his business he was thought to be a computer nerd and a weirdo. He begged people to partner with him. Some laughed at him but, a few bought into his idea, and those who bought into his business are now multimillionaires. Bill Gates needed a partner.

I was just in Springdale, Arkansas, near Bentonville, the headquarters of Wal-Mart. Practically everybody there works at Wal-Mart. There are stories by the dozens of Mr. Walton's wanting someone to loan him $10,000 so he could get started. He went around in his pickup truck begging the banks and others to help him. A few people decided to help him get off the ground. Those people are multimillionaires many times over by investing just $10,000. The rest of the crowd is like the crowd in Atlanta that could have bought into Coca-Cola and did not. The landscape is full of these fellows who missed a golden opportunity. You can hear old timers say, "My grandfather could have bought Coca-Cola stock for a nickel a share." They had an opportunity but did not take it.

God has always looked for partners. One of our missionaries is an orthopedic surgeon. She is in West Africa living in an African village. She runs an African hospital. She gave up a good practice in Memphis to go down there and live in an African village. Recently we had to bring her home to rest. She had performed sixty-four major surgeries with not more than two hours of sleep between surgeries. Forty-four of those surgeries were life-threatening. She finally collapsed, and we had to bring her home. She is making crippled children walk. She is giving people who do not have a chance to live, that chance. God could make crippled children walk without her, but he usually chooses someone to join hands with him as his partner. I could spend weeks giving you testimony after testimony of how God has used mortals to do the supernatural. God could do anything himself. He does not have to have our help, but there is something about him that will not allow him to do most of the work that is done on earth without a human partner. That is why you and I are in the ministry. God has chosen us to be co-laborers with him, to be workers with him to get his work done on earth.

The Book that Changed Everything

This book came into my possession in the most remarkable way. After I read it, I knew I wanted to use it to convey the dimensions of the spiritual struggle involved in Bible translation. Before I got into the work of Bible translation, I thought I knew the devil. Since I have been in this work, I have discovered that in all the previous years I had only a nodding acquaintance with him. I know him a lot better now. He hates the Word. God loves the Word. He said he would honor his Word above his name. The opposite of that love of God for the Word is Satan's hatred of the Word. This book entitled *God Spoke Tibetan* is the story of the ninety-year struggle to give the Tibetan people the Bible in their mother tongue. Ninety years! Two men went to Tibet as missionaries and soon decided that if they were ever going to stabilize a church there and nurture the new converts, they must have the Word. They thought it would take only a short time. They died some twenty years later, and their work had just begun.

During that time a Tibetan Lama, a prince, had become a Christian and decided that he would help them. He had renounced riches to give his life to helping them, so he took up the work and continued it. At one point when they sent the manuscripts over a high mountain pass, the man that was carrying the manuscripts in a pouch on a horse's back was caught in a terrible thunderstorm. The lightening was so severe that it killed the horse. The saddle was burned, but the manuscripts were not touched, even though the rider was deaf the remainder of his life. It was like hell roared against those manuscripts to burn them, but God said, "No!"

Later, when the manuscripts were ready to go to England for publication, the war broke out. They were stored in the basement of a church in London. A 500-pound German bomb fell within feet of where the manuscripts were stored, but the bomb did not explode. God protected his Word. Decade after decade, this struggle went on. Finally, the manuscripts were taken back to India. Missionaries were helping by now, and they brought the Tibetan down the mountain to continue his work. The temperature was 105–110 degrees, and since the Tibetan was used to living high in the mountains, the heat was killing him. He fainted; he was sick; he begged to go back to his mountains. Finally, he told the people with whom he was working that he would die if he could not get back to the high altitudes. Just then that genius of the Holy Spirit broke through, and the missionary had an inspiration. He went down to the icehouse, bought a truckload of ice, came back and built a wall of fifty-pound ice cubes. He sat that old Tibetan inside that cubicle and turned on an electric fan. This continued as the old man worked on the manuscripts.

Finally, the Bible was published, and eleven days after it was published the old Tibetan, who had worked on it so many years, died. It was as if God had kept him alive to finish his work. It had been ninety years since the task had begun. Soon thereafter, the Chinese communists invaded Tibet. The Tibetan monasteries were torn down, their priests mutilated, and everything was in an upheaval. Then the generals and political commissars from China who had conquered Tibet discovered they had a problem. They could not speak the Tibetan language.

The Christians were saying, "Why this waste? After ninety years we finally have a Bible in our own language. Now it is costing some of us our heads. The Bible is being confiscated. They are killing Christians that own a Bible. Why? We get a Bible, and then the Chinese communists come." The Tibetans did not understand. The generals discovered that they would have to teach all their troops how to speak Tibetan if they were going to rule this land. The only way to teach an unknown language is to take a manuscript of a known language and put it down beside the unknown. The only two books in the world with identical texts in Chinese and Tibetan was God's Word. So, Chairman Mao's troops, generals, majors, colonels, captains, and sergeants sat in classrooms day after day reading Matthew, Mark, Luke, John, and the book of Acts.

In early 1976, I resigned the church that I had pastored for several years and set about to organize a missions ministry that is now known as Evangel Bible Translators. From the beginning, the basic purpose of the new organization would be to translate, publish, and distribute God's Word for people who had never had the scriptures in their own language. A few days after my farewell service at the church, I received a message from a family that had been very much a part of our ministry for a number of years. The father of the family had died, and they requested that I conduct his funeral. While waiting for the final arrangements to be made and the funeral service to begin, I met and visited with the Reverend George Vanderman, a relative of the deceased, who had been asked by the family to participate in the funeral service.

Rev. Vanderman had for many years been very well known in America as the person who presented a powerful and interesting television broadcast entitled "It Is Written." He was curious as to why I would leave the church and start a new missionary organization from scratch.

I welcomed the opportunity to explain to him that God had sovereignly called me to lead an emphasis on Bible translation among the Christians of my circle of influence, that I had embraced that call, and that the vision had become the passion of my life. As I shared with joy and enthusiasm what I knew to be the will of God for the rest of my life, suddenly he said to me, "There's a wonderful book that you must read. I will send you a copy." In a few days, a beautifully bound book entitled *God Spoke Tibetan* arrived in the mail. I read the book with a great deal of interest. Little did I realize that this fascinating book would play a vital part in my future ministry. And little did I realize that God would use the story that the book contained to mold my life to touch the lives of thousands of people, to enlighten many, many people to what it means to be a Bible translator.

After I read this book that so clearly and powerfully portrays the struggle and the triumph of those who endeavored to give God's word to people for the first time in their own language, I sent a copy of the book to Pat Robertson, founder of the *700 Club* television ministry. I was invited to appear on the program to tell this wonderful story. I accepted the invitation to be a guest on the *700 Club*, and put the date on my calendar. I was very busy in those days, but I was quite proud of my ability to manage my calendar and to be punctual, and to keep appointments. However, somehow I had overlooked the date that I was supposed to be in Virginia Beach to appear on the *700 Club* television program. To my utter astonishment and horror, I discovered one day that I was supposed to be in Virginia Beach the next morning at eight to appear on the program. It was noon in southern California;

there seemed no way to get from southern California to Virginia Beach in that time frame.

It was too late to schedule a flight, but God gave me an idea. I checked with Delta Airlines and found a late night flight from Los Angeles to Atlanta. I remembered that my friend, Bob Smith, in Birmingham, Alabama, owned a manufacturing company that had a corporate airplane, and I felt free to call on him to help me. I called him and told him that I needed his plane to meet me in Atlanta the next morning at four and take me to Virginia Beach. He said, "Our company plane flies on company business every day, but, amazingly, tomorrow it is not scheduled to fly, and the pilot is standing by waiting for me to give him instructions. I will call and tell him to fly to Atlanta in the morning." He made arrangements for us to meet, and at four the next morning I jumped off the big jet, hailed a cab to take me to the other side of the airport where the private plane was waiting, boarded, and off we went to Virginia Beach. I arrived at the *700 Club* with ten minutes to spare. Somehow, God helped me to be fresh and alert and able to tell the story on the television program as they had requested. Then I went to the hotel and collapsed.

Viewing the program that day in upstate New York was a lady in her mid to late eighties who had served as a missionary on the border of Tibet for forty-plus years. She was back in America, retired, and watching the *700 Club* that morning and heard me tell the story that is in the book, *God Spoke Tibetan*. A few days later I received a letter from this veteran missionary requesting a copy of the book, which I gladly sent to her. After she read the book, she wrote me another letter telling me that she thought she knew the descendants of the man whose story is told in this book, and she said, "I am going to do the detective work to see if I can find his descendants."

Considerable time passed—several months—and then I received another letter from her telling me that she had found the grandson of Joseph Gergan, the central figure in the story, and that the grandson, Elijah Gergan, was a seminary student in South Korea. She gave me his address and I immediately corresponded with him. We began to build a friendship by correspondence, and eventually Elijah Gergan, the grandson, came to southern California at our invitation and was a guest in our home for three weeks. Elijah told us that he knew that his grandfather was a Bible translator but he knew little else. He had welcomed the book about his grandfather and had sent a copy of the book to his father who was a professor of Tibetan History and Culture in a prestigious university in Germany. The father said that the book about the grandfather was amazingly accurate.

Because of the testimony that is written in this book and our conversations with Elijah, and because of Elijah's knowledge of the spiritual needs of the Tibetan people, he made a commitment to God and to us to continue the work that his grandfather had begun in 1855. Elijah returned to northern India, where he lives on the border of Tibet, to continue his ministry to the Tibetan people who live in that vast region. There he would help us spearhead an effort to reproduce the New Testament and to produce an Old Testament in the Tibetan language. Later Elijah married the daughter of a Nepalese who was involved in translating a Bible in one of the Nepalese languages. At this point, the story was slowly beginning to unfold, and our involvement in it was beginning to come into focus.

While a guest speaker at a missions convention in Florida, the host pastor asked me to tell the congregation about Tibet and the story that is in this book. I told the story, and in the congregation was a delegation of ladies who had been to Haiti on a mission trip. I learned later that they came to the service rather reluctantly because they were exhausted, and felt that the last thing they needed to do was to go to a missionary service. I talked about what God was doing for Tibet and what he was doing in my life in regards to Tibet. We did not know at the time that these ladies had an intercessory prayer group that was dedicated to praying for Tibet and that this group had been in intercessory prayer for many years on behalf of the spiritual needs of the people of Tibet.

A few days later, after having read this book, these ladies requested a copy of the Tibetan New Testament. Their interest had been heightened considerably, and they wanted a copy of the New Testament in the Tibetan language. At first, I refused to send it to them because I had what I thought was the only copy and what probably still is the only copy in North America of the New Testament in the Tibetan language. I teasingly said to them, "If I loan you my precious book you will probably spill gravy on it." We laughed about it, but I did eventually send them the book, and they did proceed to spill gravy on my treasured book. Why would they want a Tibetan Bible that they could not read?

They called me again, still very mysterious and secretive. They asked, "Where is the Gospel of John in this Tibetan New Testament?"

I told them that I could not read Tibetan and could not tell them. Even while I was talking to them it occurred to me that in the book, *God Spoke Tibetan*, there is perhaps a third of a page where John 3:16 is printed in Tibetan allowing the people who read this book to see how difficult it is to write and read the Tibetan language. I said to them, "I think if you take the book and carefully match the text in the book with the text in the New Testament, you will be able to locate John 3:16, and once you locate this verse, you can very easily identify where the Gospel of John begins and ends in this book."

Weeks went by and another call came saying, "We thought you would like to know that we did find the Gospel of John in the Tibetan New Testament and we have taken it upon ourselves to print 5000 copies of the Gospel of John, and we are going to take them to Tibet." They said that they could take only 4000 copies to Tibet, so they would send me 1000 copies.

I said to them, "You can't go to Tibet. Tibet is closed." I continued, "You can't go there."

These ladies said, "Well, we did not know that, so we prayed over three members of our group, and they left yesterday to go to Tibet." A few weeks later they called to tell me the happy story of how they did succeed in getting into China and making their way across China into Tibet where they delivered 4000 copies of the Gospel of John.

To get 4000 copies of the Gospel of John into Tibet, a land closed and forbidding, was a major achievement. We later learned that these ladies, in their zeal and simple approach to doing things for God, had gone into Buddhist temples in Tibet. Noticing that the monks who were spinning the prayer wheels and burning incense would pull off their chiffon orange-colored outer robes and hang them in what we would call a cloakroom or closet at the entrance to the temple, the ladies would slip into the entry way where the robes were hanging and put copies of the Gospel of John into the pockets of the robes, while the monks were praying their Buddhist prayers in the inner part of the temple. When the priests would come out of their prayer time and put on their robes they would find this strange book in their pockets. "…faith cometh by hearing, and hearing by the Word of God" (Romans 10:17).

The Transition

I had been a guest on *Huntley Street*, the Canadian television program which is much like the *700 Club* television program in the United States, and I had been asked to tell the story about the book, *God Spoke Tibetan*. One of the interviewers was the wife of a newscaster who was stationed in Jerusalem. This was the beginning of a friendship with the newscaster and his wife. One day while at Evangel Bible Translator's missions orientation school in Wisconsin, I received a call from this newscaster in Jerusalem. He said to me, "I have been employed by the United States Chamber of Commerce and the Chinese government to take a delegation of VIPs and business leaders from America into China, and we think there is a very good possibility that we may get to go to Tibet. I remember the story you told when my wife interviewed you. I read the book that you gave her, and I was just wondering if there are any copies of the Gospel of John or New Testaments in the Tibetan language that we could take with us. My television crew will be traveling with this group of VIPs. Because we are guests of the communist government of China, we will not be examined too closely at the border, and there is a good chance that we can get gospel literature into China along with our cameras and television equipment."

In the meantime, I had been in India and had met with Elijah Gergan, the grandson of Joseph Gergan. While riding in a taxi one day in Bangalore, he and I saw the Bible Society's warehouse. I said to him, "I wonder if, by chance, any of the original 5000 New Testaments printed in the Tibetan language so long ago could be stored away somewhere in the Bible house." He went into the Bible house and inquired, but they told him that there were no New Testaments there and if there were any of the original 5000 remaining they would be in the warehouse in Calcutta.

A few days later we were in Calcutta. Elijah went to the Bible house, and again he was told there were no New Testaments there in the Tibetan language. Elijah said to the manager of the Bible house, "Would you please give me your permission to go into the warehouse to see if I can find any of these New Testaments that were printed in 1949?" He went on to say, "You know, they could have been here so long that they could have just been lost, and you might not even know what a New Testament in Tibetan looks like. If you would be kind enough to let me go look, maybe I could find some." The manager of the warehouse gave permission to Elijah to go in and look for these New Testaments. He found 1100 of the original 5000 New Testaments stored in this Calcutta warehouse, and they had been there over forty years. They were in good condition and were for sale. We made arrangements to buy all 1100 of these New Testaments in the Tibetan language. I then had in my possession 1100 complete New Testaments in the Tibetan language. I also had 1000 copies of the Gospel of John in California, and I had a television crew who had volunteered to take these precious books into Tibet through China. Now, when I say that I had 1100 of these New Testaments in my hand, that was not quite accurate. We knew where they were, we had control of them, but they were still in Calcutta.

I learned that a brother in Christ was making a trip from Israel to Canada, and from Canada he would be going to San Francisco, then to Hong Kong and into Tibet. By the time I learned of his trip, he was already on a plane flying from Jerusalem to Canada. I had to somehow arrange for the New Testaments that were in my office in Orange, California, to meet the plane in San Francisco. Also, I knew that getting 1100 New Testaments from Calcutta to Hong Kong would be quite a challenge, logistically. I worked all night by telephone calling my friends in Hong Kong and India, insisting that they help me to get the 1100 Bibles on a British Airways flight leaving Calcutta that night and arriving in Hong Kong in time for the Bibles to be transferred to my friend and his television crew. The Evangel Bible Translators staff in California succeeded in getting the Gospel of John copies to San Francisco. The television crew picked them up there and took them on to Hong Kong. My friends in Calcutta were able to deliver 1100 New Testaments to Hong Kong, and a television crew that I have never met to this day put these New Testaments in with their gear and equipment and was able to get them across the border into China, and on to Tibet where they delivered them. The manager of this television crew called me later and told me that when they were about to cross the border into China, the president of the Bank of America picked up the suitcases with the copies of the Gospel of John and transported them across the border into China. It was a wonderful victory for all of these Bibles to be brought together and successfully smuggled into China, and taken across China and into Tibet.

A few weeks later, I was eating lunch in a hotel in Dallas when a well-dressed lady came over to my table, introduced herself, and asked me if I were Syvelle Phillips, the founder of Evangel Bible Translators. I told her that I was, and she said, "I went to China a few weeks ago as a tourist, and at the last minute I was permitted to go into Tibet. While in Tibet, we visited the Buddhist temples. There we found copies of the Gospel of John in the hands of Buddhist monks who were reading them avidly." She said, "I know the Gospels were well-read because they were dirty and showed signs of having been used." It was a wonderful confirmation to me that these New Testaments and the copies of the Gospel of John had been successfully delivered to Tibet, and they were being read by the monks who spin the prayer wheels in the Buddhist temples.

Sometime later, I received a letter, postmarked in Australia, from a person I did not know and had never heard of. He explained to me that his forefathers and other members of his immediate family had served for over forty years as missionaries to Tibet. They had been permitted to live in a valley in the far extreme eastern corner of Tibet and had lived there forty years. They had returned to Europe old and exhausted, and had lived only a few years after their return. Before their deaths, they had written letters to their descendants, who were then living in Australia. These letters contained a diary or history of their work in Tibet, and told of very important documents stored in a trunk in the basement of a house located in a valley in a remote part of Tibet. These letters authorized the grandchildren and the great grandchildren to retrieve these documents, if the old missionaries themselves were not able to go back to Tibet and get them.

Of course, the old missionaries died before they were able to return to Tibet. The family members were intrigued. They wondered what was in the trunk, and they were writing to ask me if I knew anyone in Tibet or associated with Tibet. I responded to this letter, giving them the address of Elijah Gergan, the grandson of Joseph Gergan. They corresponded with him, and eventually sent him a copy of the letter and the documents that their deceased missionary fore parents had given them. Elijah took their letter, which authorized him to retrieve the contents of a trunk that was hidden in the basement of an ancient house in a remote valley in

Tibet. He and his father went to this house, introduced themselves, showed the old lady who owned the house the letter, and she readily agreed for them to go into the basement and retrieve the trunk and its contents. In the trunk that had been there well over forty years were a hymnbook and five hand-written Tibetan New Testaments that were leather-bound and carefully preserved. These documents were in excellent condition.

As Elijah and his father visited with the lady who was in her eighties, they learned that she was packing to move from her home because of her age and health, and that within the next two weeks the house would be torn down. God's timing is always precise! Later when I was in India, Elijah brought me a copy of one of those hand-written New Testaments and gingerly laid it in my hands. I held it and stared at it in awe and said to Elijah, "What does it mean for us to find these hand-written, leather-bound New Testaments that have been written in yet another Tibetan dialect?" This was a dialect separate and distinct from the main Tibetan language. Apparently, these missionaries had written a few verses each day as part of their daily devotions. We believe they labored about thirty years writing a New Testament. Each member of the family had hand-written his own copy. These leather-bound, hand-written Bibles were stored in a trunk, and God had supernaturally preserved them all of these years, and there I was holding one in my hand, asking Elijah what it meant. He said, "It means that another language group in Tibet has a Bible written in their own language, and it is available to be printed."

Later, I was a guest on a television program in El Paso and again told this story. After the program was over, one of the technicians came running to me with tears streaming down his cheeks and said, "I know what you are saying is true, because I worked in that valley installing a telephone system for one of the World Bank organizations, and I met the descendants of the converts of these old missionaries. We rejoiced together as he shared this unusual story.

While this story that began in 1855 is not complete, because Tibet remains in the grip of the forces of darkness, progress is being made. Elijah Gergan is now the pastor of a congregation of more than 200 believers. More than 1000 children attend a Christian school. There are Tibetan orphanages and schools in north India and Nepal that minister to the needs of Tibetan children. Thousands of Christians now travel to Tibet each year to participate in intercessory prayer walks to witness and distribute Christian literature.

The Early Years of Bible Translation

We had just completed our new sanctuary at the church I was serving in southern California, and I was so proud of it. I was in the prime of my life. I walked into that building one day alone and suddenly I was overwhelmed with the realization that any one of a hundred men could pastor that church. Maybe there was something special that God wanted done that no one had volunteered to do. That thought overwhelmed me. I walked from the entrance of that fancy new church to the old fashion altars that I had insisted on being placed in that sanctuary, and I was so taken with this idea that I found myself stretched out on top of one of those altars. I was saying to God, "God, any one of a hundred men could pastor this church. Maybe there is something special you want done that no one has volunteered to do.

Here am I, Lord, if you need me. As much as I love this church and as proud as I am of this building, if you have something you want done that no one has volunteered to do, here am I. Send me." Like most Americans, I had no knowledge of the thousands of language groups that have no scripture. I just presumed that everybody in the world had a Bible of some kind that they could read. It came to me as a shock to discover that there are hundreds of millions of people who have never read a verse of God's Word. I had a very limited understanding of this fact. Think how amazed the average Christian must be to discover that, as of this day, there are probably 4,000 different languages throughout the world in which there is no scripture.

In my association with the people from Wycliffe Bible Translators, I learned that the mayor of the city was the nephew of Uncle Cameron Townsend, the founder of Wycliffe. I met the mayor during negotiations with city government to take our church building to make it part of a civic center complex. This nephew went to Uncle Cameron Townsend and said, "I have found the man you have been praying for. He has a heart for missions. He is a young preacher. Why don't you talk to him?"

It was less than six weeks later, when Uncle Cameron Townsend sent for me. When I reached his office, he said to me, "For years we have prayed that God would raise up someone to lead an emphasis on Bible translation among your kind of people (meaning Pentecostals). You come highly recommended, and I want to challenge you to accept the responsibility for leading your kind of people in an involvement in Bible translation."

Over a period of years, Uncle Cam sowed a seed in my heart. From the first time he talked to me about providing some leadership, particularly for the young people that were coming into the church through the Jesus Movement, etc., it took me six years to come to a decision. I was not resisting. I just needed to be sure that it was God. I founded Evangel Bible Translators. We continue to have an excellent working relationship with Wycliffe.

They train all of our people. We coordinate everything we do, not only with them but with all the other major Bible translation ministries throughout the world. The task is so great and we do not want to duplicate or compete. Each of us is committed to helping the others accomplish the task.

My first response to Uncle Cam was, "Why me? Don't you see that we have boards, choirs, committees? We do what the gentiles do, and we are doing it well. Why would you bother me? I am not an educator. I am not a linguist. I am the least qualified." But somehow the idea that he placed in my mind would not go away. It became a raging fire, and I walked out of that church to start my life and ministry over. If we never start another project, and as small and weak as our effort is, 100,000,000 people will have the Word of God in their own language for the first time in the history of the world. But, thank God, we will start new projects.

Just over eleven years ago, when at the culmination of six years of God's dealing with me, I resigned my church. I was in the final throes of making that decision. Part of the price tag was leaving my denomination because they did not understand what God had called me to do; and I was at the midway point in my life and ministry and faced with some very harsh reality—like what am I going to eat? My church had given me a new Chrysler for Christmas, and I knew that when they gave me the key I could not keep it. I knew that when I left they would want it back. That is exactly what happened. Some in the church did not feel that way. However, it was a time of enormous trauma and change for us. God was leading us to provide some leadership in a type of missionary work that was not familiar to full gospel people.

For about six years prior to making this decision, I doubt if I slept all night more than a dozen times. I was up night after night praying about this whole thing. Sometimes two minutes, sometimes two hours. I was always crying out in my heart, "God, I must know! I cannot be rash about this. If you are really leading in this direction, you are not dealing with a rebel; you are dealing with a friend. My problem is not resisting your will; my problem is that I just want to be absolutely sure, not only of your will but the timing." Timing is as important as what you do. God was not dealing with someone whose will had to be broken, but one who wanted to follow closely. It was during the time that we were coming right down to the crisis when I had to say "yes" or "no."

One night I got up in the middle of the night and lay face down in the floor back in the den away from the rest of the family. I dug my hands into the carpet and cried out in agony of my soul saying to God, "I do not know any other fellowship but the church in which I am three generations deep. I do not even know any other preachers. I do not know any other churches. I have never been anywhere else. This is my tribe and my people, and if they do not understand what you are doing and where you are leading me, and if all things remain equal like I have seen it happen to others, then I will be shut out. Where will I go? Who will believe me? Who will share my vision? Who will be partners with me in this work? God, I do not know where to go. I do not know anyone else. If I walk out of this, I walk out of everything I know. I need to hear from you." That was the cry of my soul.

While lying there in the dark, my wife came in and knelt down beside me. She put her arms around me and told me how much she loved me. She said, "Apparently you are walking through waters so deep that I cannot go with you. The Lord knows I try, but I have gone as far as I can. I do not really understand what you are going through. But I believe in you, and when you pray and work your way through this, come and tell me what God's wants you to do, and we will do it together. You can depend on me." That was a tremendous ministry to me. Her expression unleashed a torrent of emotion. She kissed me, went back to bed, and left me alone with God.

In that moment God visited me in one of the most powerful visitations that I have ever experienced. God began to tell me not to be afraid. He said, "If you will go in my name, hundreds of millions of people will have the Word of God, people who have never had it. I will fight your battles. I will supply your needs. I will open doors that you do not know anything about." Then the Lord said something that I had never thought of. It could have come only from the pure heart of God. He said to me, "Do not worry about where you are going to preach or the churches you are going to visit, because I am going to supernaturally put you into relationships with pastors you have never met. You will not have to write letters or make phone calls, I will arrange it. And when I do, they will receive you, and they will make you part of their lives, and I will make them part of yours, and you will never want for a place to preach. I am going to teach you what it means to live by daily bread. If you go in faith, starting your life and ministry all over again, I will send you to churches that do not exist now except as a gleam in my eye and a dream in my heart. I am going to call them forth. They are going to be mighty churches, and they are going to need someone to help them fulfill their need to be involved in world evangelism, and I am going to send you to bless those churches and those pastors."

I had never thought of such a thing. I got up off the floor knowing that there was going to be a great wave of the Spirit of God that would bring forth churches where churches did not exist. When I was lying on that floor, Church on the Rock did not exist. I had never heard of Larry Lea. God supernaturally sent us to Dallas from California. I had never met your pastor. This church is one of those churches that did not exist, when I was lying on the floor, except as a dream in God's heart.

While going through this time of soul-searching and trying to reach a decision, I remained home one day to pray about this life-changing venture. Around 10:00 a.m., a call came from David DuPlessis, a highly respected leader in Charismatic renewal. We had met twice, and each visit was very brief. Brother David told me that he was in Europe and that while praying that morning, God spoke to him saying that he should call and encourage me to go forward with whatever I was considering to do for the Lord. He went on to say that whatever I was praying about, whatever God was leading me to do, do it now and God would be with me. This word of encouragement came from a great man of God, a man that I barely knew. I had never heard from him before and have not heard from him since. This call from a man for whom I had great respect was one more confirmation that I was to give my life without reservation to the cause of missions and Bible translation. God bless Brother David for his obedience. "Behold, to obey is better than sacrifice" (1 Samuel 15:22).

When we first opened an office, we had nothing. Another missionary organization paid half my secretary's salary. My former church gave me a six-month severance pay so my family could survive. Wycliffe Bible Translators leased an IBM typewriter for us. A Christian brother gave me a 1973 Lincoln Continental with low mileage. A family who owned a service station contributed four years of gasoline for two cars. We had no funds for a desk and chair. While having lunch with a dear brother, he asked me what I had prayed for that morning. I told him that I had prayed for a desk and chair for my office. He replied, "I have a new desk and chair that have been in storage for years. You can have them." When they were delivered, two side chairs and a new stereo came with them. Another day, a man brought an expensive mimeograph and stencil maker. Others brought adding machines, filing cabinets, and a printing press. A group of friends committed to support my family and pay my travel expenses. My radio ministry on thirteen radio stations on the West Coast generated more support.

Editor's note:

Church on the Rock was the great church built by Pastor Larry Lea in Rockwall, Texas. Syvelle and Larry met by chance at a missions conference. They had never seen each other, but Larry approached Syvelle and told him to come to his church as the first missionary speaker that they had invited to the new church. The story that you just read was told there and it tells volumes about how the Bible translation ministry was born.

Mother Tongue Speakers

One of the unique things about Evangel Bible Translators is that we have been led by the Holy Spirit to use what we call "mother tongue speakers" wherever possible. Many years ago God dealt with me like this: What if we could find a man from a tribe, educate him, train him, and send him back to his own people—a people he understands? He would know the culture and could communicate. Such a man could go back to his own people with excellent academic qualifications, excellent spiritual qualifications, and write a Bible in his own tongue for his own people.

When I first approached the leadership of Wycliff about this, Uncle Cam Townsend, the founder of Wycliff and the person who actually encouraged me to start Evangel Bible Translators, said to me, "Syvelle Phillips, you are nuts." I asked him why he would say such a thing. He said that most of the training and most of the printed material are available only in English. There is a bit in German and Swedish, but mostly English. It is an English language subject at the university level. Then he asked me, "How are you going to teach a man that comes out of a tribe from a primitive village to do such sophisticated academic work?" He again said that it could not be done. But I could not get away from that idea, and it kept burning in my spirit. I searched for two years, but could find no one. When I gave up and admitted to God that I could not find anyone, three came in one day, supernaturally. They have not stopped coming. Today we have men who have earned Ph.D. degrees working with us; some could not read until they were adults. It can be done!

I want to tell you about a young man, a native of India where he had been trained to be a Bible translator. He has now been associated with our ministry for several years. I traveled to India to meet with several of our translators. I had not seen the young man in five years. When I met him he was carrying a plastic bag, similar to a shopping bag. As he began to tell me about the progress of his work he pulled a little notebook from the bag, and in this little notebook he had translated the entire gospel of Mark, which had taken him five years. He showed me the manuscripts he had translated by hand of ten New Testament stories including the birth of Jesus, some of the healing miracles, the crucifixion, and the resurrection. He also had translated fifteen Old Testament stories.

This man had never owned a bicycle. He lived in a hut, which probably had a dirt floor. He had never even thought of owning a car. He had never ridden in an airplane. He had ridden a train. Very shyly and timidly, this young man asked me if he could have a computer. He said if he had a computer he could enter into it all of his five years of work, and with a laser printer he could produce the master copies so that the print shop could do mass printing of his material. He said he needed to print 5,000 copies of the Gospel of Mark and circulate them among the people who could read to see if they could read what he had translated and understand it.

It struck me as being awesome that a man who had never owned a bicycle and never dreamed of owning a car would ask for a computer. I said to him, "If you had a computer, could you use it?"

He replied, "Yes sir!" He told me that he had ridden the train for two days to reach Bangalore, a large city in southern India where the computer industry of India is concentrated, to learn how to use the computer. Some Indian brothers there had a ministry of teaching computer science to men like this young man.

He then reached into his shopping bag and pulled out a piece of brown cardboard that looked like the lid off a box. Those fellows in Bangalore had drawn a mock keyboard of a computer on the cardboard and taught him where to place his fingers. He had been practicing his finger movements on this mock keyboard in faith that God would give him a computer to use. I was awestricken at what was transpiring before my eyes. A friend, who had just retired from United Airlines, was with me. I looked at my friend and saw him weeping. He said, "Pastor Phillips, get this man a computer and I will bring it to him." A few days later I received a fax from India telling me that the computer had been delivered. This young man went back to Bangalore to receive additional instructions in the use of computers, and to learn how to use the software.

God has lead us in a most remarkable way to believe, by the grace of God, that men who come from these tribes can be educated academically, theologically, and spiritually to move into the computer age and use the latest equipment to give their own people the Word of God.

The Work of Translation

The questions I am most often asked about Bible translation are: "How do you go about translating a Bible?" and "If people of a language group cannot read, what good does it do to give them a Bible?" I want to try to address both of these questions. When a Bible translator goes to live with a language group that has no written language, one of the first things he must pray for is a person—a friend and helper—in that village or town or language group to help him with his work. Our missionaries are encouraged to pray that God will give them a local person to whom their hearts can be knit. That person will be a key to helping the missionary learn the language and culture, and gain favor with the people. The Bible translator begins his work by collecting words, a tedious process. The translator is highly trained, and his ears are sensitive to what he hears. He builds a dictionary of words and their meanings. He continues word-by-word, sentence-by-sentence until he can speak the language, and has a good understanding of how that language flows—the pitch, the tone, the definitions, and the meanings. Then he begins writing simple stories. He can begin teaching the people even while he is learning.

A well-managed Bible translation project often has a team of several people working together. Beginning with very elementary teaching the natives are taught to read what is being written in their language. As you can imagine, this process is difficult and requires a long time to complete. Those of us who serve the Lord and believe in the enabling ministry of the Holy Spirit can trust God to make the jobs, which sound so difficult and impossible, possible with his help and with the good linguistics training that is available to our missionaries. It is not an impossible task. It can and is being done in a most remarkable way.

One of our couples went to the Philippines twenty-nine years ago to live in a community of 350,000 people who had no written language. There were, of course, no schools, no books, no Bible, no hymnbooks—nothing. They have completed the translation of the New Testament and have made great progress in translating the Old Testament. As they worked on the New Testament they trained young people there to help. Much of their time has been spent in teaching adults and children to read as the materials have been developed. They say to the people who want to learn to read, "I will not charge you any money to teach you to read, but you must promise that if I teach you to read you will teach five other people to read." That is a wonderful system.

There is a joint effort between many of the Bible societies and translation agencies to work together to teach people to read. The larger ministries produce Bible stories illustrated like comic books. These are printed in enormous volumes leaving the words out of the bubble. Our people order these preprinted comic book-like stories and fill in the language bubbles. People love this method of teaching. They learn the story and the Bible truth while at the same time learning to read.

The work of Evangel Bible Translators isn't just about getting Bibles written, printed, and distributed. It is also about helping to meet a fundamental need—literacy. Literacy rates are generally very low in the areas where our translators work. In many cases, no written language has ever existed. So, beyond the challenges of meeting spiritual needs, the work of Bible translation offers opportunities to meet educational, social, and cultural needs. In many cases our Bible stories have been used to teach people to read and write. When people learn to read and write, they become more effective and productive participants in education, the economy, and the society.

Bible translation is a very demanding and long-term ministry, taking up to thirty years to translate the Bible. I do not have long lines of people at my office wanting to do this work, but wonderful people do come. They respond to the sovereign dealing of the Holy Spirit in their lives. Our role is to encourage them, help them get the training they need, help them raise the finances, and help them get the computer equipment they need. I am somewhat of a pastor—a father figure—to these dedicated and gallant young people whom I call the Green Berets of the church. I visit them. I pray with them. I weep with them. I am there to help them when emergencies and trials come.

When one of our translators died, it was my privilege to stand with the young wife and teenage children and love them and minister to them while they were going through that horrible ordeal. They work in a remote area where there is no church.

We need prayer partners. We need money. We need a lot of good will. I am really pleased to have the privilege of touching a heart by raising the curtain a bit and saying, "Hey, Americans, there is a world out there that does not walk on carpet or live in air-conditioned and centrally heated homes. There are people out there who do not have an abundance of food to the point that its people need a diet. There are hundreds of thousands of people out there who cannot read John 3:16, and who have never heard a hymn. What a joy it is to give those people the Word of God in their own language! We need the prayers of people who have a tender heart for the work of God. We need young people to train. We need retired people who will give their time. It is not the type of ministry that one person can do alone. It is an enormous and wonderful undertaking.

I have been with 400 pastors in one meeting where only one could read and write. What a privilege to know that if we are faithful in our efforts and continue to make ourselves available to God, we can make it possible not for just a few preachers but for an entire language group to have the Word of God in their own language. One of the tools we have used to help ministers who have churches but no Bible to read is a solar-powered cassette machine. The sun charges the batteries. We ask native (mother tongue) speakers to read the scriptures onto tapes, and these tapes are given to pastors who cannot read. By listening to these tapes, they hear the Word of God in their own language. That has been a tremendous tool to make the Word available to people who have not yet learned to read, or for people who will never learn to read.

When I was starting Evangel Bible Translators, I was in a Bible college in northern California speaking for the chapel service. While I was speaking, the glory of God came down in a powerful and supernatural manifestation of God's presence. In fact, I do not know that I have ever seen anything quite like it before or since. Probably 300 students and faculty were involved. At a point in my message, people started falling out of their chairs. The ones that did not fall got out of their chairs and fell on their knees. I was the only one left standing. Faculty and students were flat on their faces, not in a swoon, but in an attitude of prayer. It was powerful, and God was obviously touching people. I ended up lying on the floor with my head under a chair praying. This prayer meeting lasted over five hours. Classes were dismissed for the day.

During that time, the Lord really spoke to my heart about how people go to college, seminary, or Bible school and come out with a good deal of head knowledge but very little of the deep things of God. I do not say this to criticize those institutions, because they are educational institutions, but what the Lord was speaking to me about was that people ought to go to the mission field with a fresh touch of God on their lives. It kept coming to me that missionary candidates ought to face reality versus the romance. Facing the real situation does not equal unbelief. It equals positioning yourself so that God can help you through the difficult times.

The original vision remains and that is to invite some of the best teachers and most experienced people we can find to give insight to our missionaries about everyday life on the field. We do this in small groups. We are fully aware that we cannot cover all the subjects, but what we can do is provoke them to think and pray and do research and begin the process whereby God can condition them spiritually, emotionally, mentally, and physically to become fruitful as quickly as possible in another culture. We have seen marvelous results. In fact, some of the people who were with us, perhaps fifteen years ago, in Wisconsin encouraged me to continue this training. They said, "We listen to the tapes. Sometimes when we splash against the wall we back up and begin reminding each other of what someone said in the training sessions." All of this was born, not of some committee, but by a sovereign dealing of the Holy Spirit that God has seen fit to honor.

Near Death

After a strenuous trip to Peru, I was not well when I arrived home. Four days after arriving home from Peru, I had to go to Dallas to take care of business. I got off the plane still not feeling well, and by ten that night, I was in the emergency room of the hospital. For the next ten days, I lay between life and death with as many as eight doctors working over me. When they discovered that I had been in the jungles of Peru that set off an alarm. Tropical disease specialists were called in. My body was swollen to twice its normal size. When my wife finally got there she found me bloated, swollen, and my skin a greenish, yellowish color. I had tubes and hoses everywhere. My doctor said to me, "There is no point in playing games with you. You are a strong man, and we might as well talk to you about your condition. Reverend, you are in big trouble, and we cannot find out what is wrong. We are going to prep you for surgery, and if you do not get better shortly we will have to do exploratory surgery."

At first they thought I had cancer. Then they thought I had an infection in my pancreas. To this day I have not had a definite diagnosis. My wife called a prayer meeting across America. Thousands of people prayed for me on a Wednesday night. Thursday morning the doctor walked into the room and said, "I do not know what happened to you during the night, but it is wonderful. The crisis is over." He started pulling out the hoses and tubes, and two days later I went home still not knowing what had happened to me. I was not able to go back to California at that time. Friends of ours took me into their gorgeous home and kept me for four or five weeks. Every night, I would sweat until the bed linens would have to be changed two or three times. It was a cold, putrid, clammy, smelly sweat that must have been the body's effort to eliminate the poisons.

During this terrible time, I never once doubted my salvation. I never once doubted my call to preach or my call to missions, but I felt that God was a million miles away. It seemed so strange that I could pray for other people and great things would happen. I would pray for myself and nothing would happen. It will mess up your theology to pray for a fellow that is down on his hands and knees yelping like a dog because his back is out of joint and God heals him instantly and you have the same problem and you do not get healed. I prayed for a fellow one night and he was healed. Sunday morning I went to church wearing a body brace. The guy who was healed the night before picked me up and danced me all over the lobby of the church glorifying God for his healing. I was screaming, "Put me down! You are killing me!" When I would stand in the pulpit and preach I would be anointed. When I was alone, the heavens were brass and there was no word from the Lord. This dragged on month after month.

Christians can be quite judgmental, when you are going through a long, dark valley. They have discernment and revelation, and they know exactly what is wrong. One fellow, whose name you would know if I mentioned it, a prolific author and a nationally known religious figure, said to me as we had breakfast together one morning, "Pastor, since there is no one here but you and me, you can confess your sin to me and tell me why God is not healing you." There was no sin in my life like he was talking about, but if I had followed the urge to slap, there could have been. He will never know what a close call or a miraculous deliverance he had.

At that time, I had a radio program that was heard all up and down the west coast, and I guess it kind of seeped through that I was going through a difficult time, and some lady sent me a dollar to buy a copy of Brother Hagan's book. She said if I would just read it I would have faith to believe for my healing. People prophesied, discerned, rebuked, and revived. Many thought there had to be something wrong. Yes, there was something wrong, but I did not know what it was. I had cried and prayed. I had repented of everything I knew to repent of. I questioned God, but the heavens were still brass; and the crazy thing was when I stood to preach, God blessed. When I prayed for other people, God blessed. But when I was alone, nothing happened. That is an ordeal and a long night of the soul, especially when you have enjoyed a close, intimate, and friendly relationship with God. How long, O Lord? What lessons must be learned?

Translators

If you are going to operate a Bible translation ministry, you will need men dedicated to the work of translation. The typical approach is to recruit and train Caucasian missionaries, and send them to foreign places to do the work. I was convinced that it would work much better to find and train men from the people groups who needed a Bible. For two years, I advertised on radio, television, and in magazines but found no one. Eventually I said to God in desperation, "I have done everything I know to do to find natives interested in this kind of work, but I have found none. I am going to stop traveling and spending money in an effort to find these men. I am going to wait on you, God. If this concept is from you, you will bring these men to me." Then came a spiritual breakthrough. In one day, three men came to me expressing an interest in translating the Bible into their languages. To this day men have never stopped coming. When we get one or two educated, others appear. I never solicit. I never recruit. God sends them.

I found myself in this little tiny church north of Dallas in a storefront with about thirty-five people in the congregation. At the end of the service, we gathered around the altar for prayer. I have to make a confession. I am super conservative about gift ministries. A lot of what I have seen and heard is baloney. I am a believer, and I am a third generation Pentecostal, but I am kind of slow sometimes.

While we were praying, the little pastor came over to me and placed his hands on my head. Of all things, he started prophesying over me, the doubting Thomas. The Holy Spirit said to me, "You hold still. This one is real."

I said, "Yes, sir."

This little fellow did not know anything about me or what I was doing or what I was thinking or what I was going through. He said, "Thus saith the Lord, I am going to give you keys to the nations."

When he said that I broke into tears, threw up my hands and instinctively knew that it meant men. I cried out to God to give me a key to Thailand, India, and Africa. The next morning I preached in the chapel service at Christ for the Nations to about 1800 students and asked if any of them wanted to be a Bible translator. The first three men in the line were from Thailand, India, and Africa!

I went to my room with my head spinning. As I walked through, the door the phone rang and it was the wife of the pastor of the big church that I had thought about while on the platform of the little church. Actually, I wondered why I was not preaching at the big church. She said, "We have heard of you and your ministry, but my husband and I have never met you. Could we take you to lunch today?"

At lunch, I told them about the prophecy in the meeting the day before. I mentioned that the brother from India was a Nepalese and lived in north India. When I said, "Nepal," this lady started shaking like a leaf.

She said, "I am sorry, but the Spirit of the Lord is on me." Tears started pouring down her cheeks, and she said, "When I was twenty and in Bible college, one day during an intercessory prayer time, God laid Nepal on my heart. I never got to go. My husband and I got married and began our ministry. We built this church and have been here for many years. I am seventy years old now, and I have always grieved that I did not get to fulfill the stirring I had about that part of the world. When you mentioned that man's name and where he was from, the same spirit that was on me fifty years ago came upon me again." She continued to shake and could not eat. She said, "I do not know what it means, but I think it means that God is going to let me fulfill the destiny that he assigned to me fifty years ago. She reached into her purse, got her checkbook, and wrote me a check for one year's tuition for the young man to attend the University of Texas to study linguistics. That man completed a translation of the New Testament in the language that we sent him to work on. That church paid for his entire education, and a New Testament is now available to a group of people who have never had the Word of God in their language.

God gave me exactly what I asked for; one from Thailand, one from India, and one from Africa! After these three men were educated and trained, more came. I have not run another ad. I have not done another interview. I have not tried to recruit another person, but the stream has never ceased. One, two, or three come, and we educate them. It is incredible that sharp, well-educated, and wonderful people keep coming.

Afghanistan

One day the phone rang. The lady on the other end of the line said, "Pastor Phillips, you do not know me but I know you. You are that Bible translator. I see you at our church every now and then. I work in an office in downtown Dallas, and a lady works with me who is from Afghanistan. She says that her husband is a Bible translator, and he would like to meet you."

In a few days, this Afghan came into my office. He was well-dressed and in his mid-fifties. I asked him to sit down and tell me his story. He said, "I was educated at the University of Oklahoma. During the four years I was in Oklahoma, no one ever once mentioned Jesus to me. When I completed my degree, I went back to Afghanistan where I got a job working with my government. Later I accepted a job with the US government." He continued, "When the war started in my country, I was thought to be a CIA agent. I really was not, but my life was on the line, and the American government got me out in the nick of time. They brought me here to the States in appreciation for the years of service that I had rendered, and gave me permission to live here." He said, "I went back to Oklahoma City because that was familiar territory, but I could not get a job there so I drifted down to Dallas. Some teenagers witnessed to me on the street and led me to the Lord. They gave me a Bible, and I read that wonderful book. It is not like the Koran. I said, 'My people have never read this book. I wish my people could read this book. Why has someone not written this book in my language?' And then the Spirit of God said to me, 'Why don't you write it?' So, every waking moment I have spent translating the Bible into the language of my people."

He reached into his briefcase and removed a little book—the Gospel of John. He said, "I have written the Gospel of John in my language. Before I came here, I had 10,000 copies printed right under the government's nose, and most of them were distributed in Iran. I got a few of them into Afghanistan. I know that I do not have all the training I should have even though I am a well-educated man. Will you help me get the training I need so I can do a better job? My life's ambition is to finish a Bible in the language of my people."

The beauty of the story I just told you is many fold, but there is one thing I do not want you to miss. God loved me enough that in the most miraculous way you could imagine he let a man come into my life, sit down in my office, and assure me that a project that I had previously sponsored did not go down the drain because of a mistake we might have made, or because one family had a heartbreaking disaster. It was like God said, "Syvelle has grieved about that long enough. He needs comfort." When that man left my office, the burden lifted. My wounded heart was healed.

Editor's note:

> A couple, sponsored by Syvelle, had attempted a project to translate a Bible for this same group of people, but had failed due to sick children and other difficulties.

China

I have made two trips to mainland China. I went to China because I had been interested in the fifty-two ethnic language groups in China that do not speak Chinese. Fifty of the fifty-two have no scripture. One group of Muslims is located on the far backside of China up toward the Russian border. Their population is 60,000,000. I have talked about this in meetings and even had Chinese people challenge me on the accuracy of what I was saying. I have had them come out of the crowd telling me that what I said was not true. They would say, "We all speak one language or at most two—Mandarin and Cantonese." I made a trip to China and learned where these people lived and the language spoken. On the first page of the first book I picked up it said, "We have tried to make these people learn the language of China, but we have failed completely. Now we are reversing our policy and telling everyone to speak his own language." I knew I was on the right track.

On my next trip, I was able to meet with one of the language groups and a veteran translator who had already completed five New Testaments. He was old. He had leukemia and was kept alive by the mercy of God. He would work a few hours and then sleep a few. He worked around the clock. He was hidden out in a secret place. I visited with him for about two hours and was awed by what I saw. The man who took me in to see him was taking manuscripts that had been corrected by a crew that lived in Hong Kong and picking up a batch of work from this translator and his helpers for proofreading. I asked this man, Robert Morris, a world-renowned linguist and translator how we could help him and encourage him. He leaned across the table and pointed to a young lady, one of his helpers and said, "Take her out of here, and train her to finish my job. She has worked with me ever since I started this project. I have taught her all I know. She needs formal training. I am dying with leukemia, and I know that I cannot live twenty more years to finish this project. She is the likely one to finish the job, but she needs the training."

India

When I knew I was going to India for a speaking engagement I invited all our translators in India to come and meet me at the school. Four teams of translators that work in various tribal areas in India came and joined me for this time of ministry. I made arrangements for them to stay in the same hotel where I was staying because I wanted them close to me. I would run out to the college and speak and then come back to be with my people. We had a week of wonderful fellowship. It is hard to communicate with words what happened in that atmosphere. You see, all four of these teams work in different parts of India and with different languages. They were all members of our mission but none of them knew each other. Having gone to school at different times, they had never met. They had gone to India at separate times, and they lived hundreds of miles apart. Most of them were in the same age group—young married couples with babies. One couple traveled forty hours on an Indian train, little more than a cattle car, one-way with an eight-month old baby to get there so they could enjoy that fellowship for a few days. It took another couple three days to get there. They came part of the way by train and part of the way by plane. To see these people, who pay a price we know nothing about, and to hear their stories was a humbling experience.

The first night, I asked them to come up to my room for "get acquainted" time. We arranged chairs in a circle. I had not met the wife of one of the young men. He came to the States to study medicine. He was going to earn a Ph.D. in microbiology engineering (gene-splicing). The projection was that it would take him seven years to earn his degree, but he was so brilliant that he earned his doctorate in five years at the University of Virginia. He came to America a pagan. While he was there some teenagers lead this brilliant, young medical student to the Lord on the streets in Norfolk, Virginia. They took him to a little church where he was baptized in the Holy Spirit. He decided that God had in his sovereignty called him to be a Bible translator. He put his career as a medical scientist behind him and went to the Wycliffe Bible Translators' training school in Dallas to become a Bible translator. That was where I met him. He became a member of Evangel Bible Translators, and we, with great pride and great joy, sent him off to India when he had completed his training.

He was then at a marriageable age, approaching thirty, and he wanted to be married. He had left India as a pagan, but he returned as a Christian. His family was not happy about his giving up a medical career. Families in India arrange the marriage of their children, and they are not too pleased about arranging a Christian marriage in their complex Indian culture. All of us prayed that God would work this out, because it is an enormous problem in India for a Christian young man to find a wife. He was invited to go to the school in India where Bible translators are trained. Only ten to twelve students were there. Wouldn't you know that one of the students who had been teaching school for seven years and was just about his age, attracted his attention, and they got together. They were able to overcome the caste system, the difference in the families, and the dowry requirements. As you probably know, there is a price for the bride that the groom has to pay. They got it all worked out and had a beautiful wedding. By the time of our meeting, this couple had a precious little baby. I had never met the wife or seen the baby. I did not know anything about her background, but I hoped Chris had made a good choice. I was anxious, as the papa of the ministry, to see the young lady my son had married. That is kind of how I felt about him. I had never heard him say much about her, and I did not know how to inquire, so I was more than anxious for her turn to come as we shared.

We went around the circle. Each one of us told where we were from, what God was doing in our lives, what we were doing in India, and the progress we were making. Ruth was probably number eight or ten. When her time came she lit up like a light bulb. When they were married she did not speak English, but after three years she was speaking beautiful English. She started giving a wonderful testimony about how she grew up in a small Indian village with Hindu parents. She told about how as a little girl, she would become greatly distressed when her father would offer goat sacrifices. The Hindus do this several times a year. When she would hear the pitiful bleats of the goats as their throats were cut, she would run into the house and pull the covers over her head thinking, "There must be a better god than this. There must be a god somewhere that does not require people to kill goats." Idols were on the walls of her parents' house, and she would say to her mother, "The stories about the gods that we serve tell of their immoral lives, and their many marriages and their concubines. We do not live like our gods lived. Why should we worship them?" She told us that she grew up with a hunger in her heart to know a god that was truly worthy of her worship and her service.

She continued, "As a grown young lady in college, I was still crying out to God. I got on my knees one day and said, 'If there is a god out there somewhere that is a true god, reveal yourself to me.' A cloud started moving toward me, and it was like a fog rolling in. When it filled my room, Jesus stepped out of that cloud. I had never heard his name, but he told me who he was and showed me the nail prints. He showed me his wounds. He told me that he died for me and that his sacrifice was once and for all. I was marvelously redeemed. I had never met a missionary, and I had never met another Christian, but I found Jesus, because he answered my cry. He answered my cry and he came to me.

"When my Hindu relatives, my mother especially, knew that I was a Christian, the persecutions came. They were strong and hard, and I said to Jesus, 'I cannot live this life without spiritual power that I do not have.' He came to me again in the rolling cloud. He stepped out of this cloud and I bowed before him and worshipped him. I was lost in his presence for I do not know how long. When I came to myself I was worshipping him in a language I had never heard. I had been truly baptized in the Holy Spirit!"

She went on to join a mission's organization and became the editor of their newspaper and magazine. She also taught in the high school. "During all those years," she said, "God was talking to me about being a Bible translator." She showed up at the school for the first time the day Chris showed up, and now they are married and have a little baby. They are living in a little village with no water or lights, and few other Christians. There is no church. She told us that 12,000,000 people speak that language, and that she and Chris are doing the preliminary work for a Bible translation.

The last morning we were together we took the same pattern of going around the table as we were eating and giving our prayer requests. We knew they were leaving at noon. When it came Ruth's turn she cried and said, "We do not have a church to attend. We live in a remote village and are doing preliminary work on a Bible. We have been told that there are only 150 Christians among 12,000,000 people. We do not know where they are because there is no church where we are. On Sunday mornings, we get our hymnbooks out and sing hymns together. We read the Bible and talk about the goodness of God. That is our church. Village life is so hard with the baby because there is no water or electricity. I cannot even hire a woman to help me with the laundry because we are Christians. The women are forbidden to talk to me. I am so lonely. Chris is gone sometimes for two weeks at a time out in the Bush, and I am left alone to care for the baby. There are no medical facilities. If I could just have a friend and someone to help me with the baby, that would be such a blessing. Ninety percent of my time is spent just sustaining life—gathering up the vegetables, preparing meals, etc."

Ruth voiced these feelings and desires at the breakfast table about nine in the morning. That afternoon I went back to the College; and while there, a sharp middle-aged Indian couple sought me out saying, "We heard Ruth and Chris give their testimony last night in the church. The best we can figure we live about fifty miles from them. (As it turned out it is about 500 miles.) God has spoken to our hearts that we are supposed to take care of them. They handed me their card, and I discovered that both of them were medical doctors. He said, "My wife is the doctor, and I am the pastor. I gave up my medical practice to establish a church. She keeps the clinic open. God spoke to us very clearly last night that we are supposed to be friends to that couple, and that we are supposed to minister to them and help them any way we can. Tell me what their needs are." I began to tell him what she had said that morning. He said, "I think we can take care of some of those needs. I will send two of my Christian girls from the church to be with them." I later received a letter from Chris and Ruth telling me that they have Christian girls there helping them with the baby. It is going to take that couple thirty years to complete their work. These are educated and sophisticated people living in very primitive conditions. They are paying a price, but that Book is worth it!

Several years ago, I was in the extreme northern part of India. Actually, if you look at a map of India, you will see on the east coast the famous city of Calcutta, which has 12 to 13 million miserable people in the most filthy and ungodly place you could imagine. If you go to Calcutta, and then go northeast by jet about two hours you will reach the last airport. After landing at the last airport, I traveled five hours in a four-wheel drive vehicle up into the mountains, where people were headhunters until some of them received the gospel in 1955. I was there to speak at a ministers' conference. One group of preachers at the meeting had to walk two and a half days to reach the meeting place. They told me that before the gospel came to them twenty years earlier they had never heard the name Jesus. They said, "Because we were neither Buddhist nor Hindu we worshipped our ancestors and animals. We quickly accepted the gospel. Thousands of our people were born again, and now we have one hundred churches."

The fellow talking to me said, "I am the leader of one hundred churches. Two years ago, my preachers and I started meeting on a regular basis. Once a month or once every two months, we try to get together all our pastors. We set aside a day to pray for a Bible in our language. When we went to a Bible society they would have nothing to do with us because we believe in receiving the Holy Spirit. They consider us a cult, and we have nowhere to turn." He continued, "A year ago we decided to add fasting to our prayer, praying that God would give us a Bible in our language. Twenty-two of us walked two and one half days to get to this meeting. We had never heard of your name or Evangel

Bible Translators, but last night when they introduced you as the founder of a Bible translation ministry I said, 'Oh glory to God, we are going to get a Bible now!'"

He explained to me that they had a population of 700,000 people, one hundred churches, and thousands of believers but no scripture. He said, "None of our pastors has ever read any of God's Word in their own language." He spoke excellent English, and had a master's degree in theology from the Buntain School of Theology in Calcutta, which is a very fine school, but his people had not learned to speak or read English. He was a rare young man.

I could tell from the way he was talking that he thought we would send an American there to write a Bible for them. I had to explain to him that the Indian government required that I get a special permit to come into that area, and that I had tried to go into that area two years before, but had been denied permission. This time, the government gave me a written permit to go in for ten days. I had to check in at the airport and promise them that I would fly out of there in ten days or less. I told him that we could not send an American there no matter what. I told him that if we could find a native as bright as he was, and as well educated, we could train that person to be a Bible translator.

I said, "You will have to help me find that person." He jumped out of his chair pounding his fist saying, "Oh thank you, Jesus. Oh, hallelujah! We are going to get God's Word in our language!" He would sit down and then jump up again saying, "Oh, praise God!" Then he said, "I know just the person! My brother, Jeremiah. He will complete his college training in May at the same school I attended in Calcutta. I have heard you say that you are going to Calcutta next week for your workers' conference. I am going to send Jeremiah there to see you."

Jeremiah, who looked just like his brother, showed up. He was a small guy with brown skin and did not look Indian at all, but more like Burmese or Vietnamese. He was as bright as could be, and full of joy and enthusiasm. When I finally got around to visiting with him, I found him as animated as his brother. He could not stay in his chair. He began to tell me about how he had been thinking and praying about the possibility that he could write a Bible for his people. He said, "I believe God has prepared me to write a Bible. Brother Phillips, if you will train me and tell me how to do it, you will not have to send a foreigner here. I will do it! I will do it!"

We put Jeremiah and fourteen other men like him through their first session of training, and sent them back to do their first cycle of work, collecting all the words in their tribal language so that they could create a dictionary. We gave Jeremiah a new laptop and new software to help him get started on the translation project.

I said to the preachers, "This cannot be an American project; it has to be your project. When you preachers gather food, bring food for Jeremiah. When he gets married, have all the men from the churches gather the timber from the forest and build him a house. Build the furniture he needs and set him up. He is your Bible translator, and you must honor him. You must not encumber him with all the things of sustaining life. When you go hunting, you bring him meat. When you farm, you give him vegetables. Every church should take an offering for him every month." They are the poorest of the poor. I said, "A fifty rupees offering, which equals one dollar, from each church will equal fifty dollars a month, and you can help finance this project." They were very enthusiastic about this.

I had a phone call from my California office later saying, "Jeremiah needs a printer for his computer." They have a little generator to run the computer and everything is working. Now they want to print what he has done.

Missionaries and Translators

A Hero with a Funny Name

A number of years ago I was in New York City on a hot Sunday in Harlem. You do not want to go to Harlem unless you have to. That is no place for tourists. I do not even remember why I was there. I do not remember how the pastor knew about me. I was in this predominantly black church of about two hundred people on this Sunday afternoon. Before the service began, the pastor told me that he had asked one of the men who was leaving in a few days to return to Africa to give a word of testimony. He introduced Brother Gboffua, a black brother barely shoulder high to me. He was well-dressed, very shy, and soft spoken. He began to tell the congregation about his plans to return to Liberia. He had just graduated from New York City University and was going home to Africa.

He said, "I could have a job on Wall Street or Madison Avenue in almost any institution I desired with the degree I have, but that is not what my heart is saying I should do." Later, I learned that he had a master's degree in business administration. "My heart is saying, 'Go back to Liberia,' and that is what I am going to do." He thanked the church for receiving him and allowing him to be a part of the church body for the past seven years.

He said, "When I moved to this city, I had never seen a large city, and I was afraid. I rented a room in an apartment down the street, and the first thing I did was to get on my knees and say, 'God, this city frightens me. I cannot live in this city without a church. I am just an African bush boy, and I do not even know how to go about finding a church. God, I ask you to give me a church to attend and guide me to that church.' That afternoon I went for a walk and passed by this building. The windows were open and you were singing. I recognized the songs, and I turned in. I never went to another church. God had answered my prayer. I have been here seven years while attending the university. I met Elaine here. We were married here. Our baby was born here. Our baby died here. You have been my family. Four years ago, our pastor asked me to be his assistant on a part-time basis, so I have been one of your pastors, and I love you and appreciate you. Now the time has come for me to say goodbye, and for Elaine and me to go back to my native Liberia in West Africa."

At one point he said to the pastor of the church, "Where I am going you could not come. You will never be able to come. I walked two days through mud from ankle to knee deep to get to the road to begin my journey to the capital where I would learn to read. I can eat the food, deal with the insects and the mud, because that is home. No missionary has ever been where I come from. A traveling African bush preacher came through the jungles to my village and preached Christ. Several of the young men in our village, including me, gave our hearts to the Lord. We cut down trees and built a church. One day God spoke to my heart and said, 'If you are ever going to bless my people you will need to get an education. You are going to have to learn to read and write.' Now I have completed my studies. I have a master's degree from New York City University, and I am going back to my country to build roads, schools, hospitals, and churches. I am going to push back the darkness. God is sending me back to my people."

Then he said, "My language has never been written." As far as we know, he is the only member of his tribe to ever learn to read. He said, "My people have no literature, no Bible, nothing. I have heard that there is a school somewhere in America that will teach me how to write a Bible. I want you to pray that God will help me find that school. If you will help me pray, God will help me find it. I want to take a few lessons so that I can learn to write at least a few key verses to give to my people."

There I was sitting on the platform. Man, I was on my feet. I said, "Brother, I not only know where the school is I have the key to the front door!" Our ministry gave him a scholarship, and he earned a degree in linguistics. He completed his training and was ready to return to Liberia. He arrived at the airport early on the day of his departure before the crowds came, and I met him there. Here we were, a tall white man with a heavy southern accent who grew up in the Deep South during the days of Jim Crow and segregation, and a black man from Africa sitting there talking to each other like the brothers we were. We talked excitedly about what he was going to do and how we all could work together.

I asked him what he was going to need. He said, "I am going to need a house for my wife and babies (he then had two babies), and I am going to need a vehicle with a four-wheel drive, and a winch because there are no roads. I am going to need a computer." He mentioned a number of other items that he would need. I was thinking, "You go write that Bible that you have been trained to write. Go teach your people to read. I will take care of the computer, the house, and as God helps me I will help you get the vehicle you need." Then the crowds came, and the plane came and it was time to say goodbye. We stood and hugged each other and wept without any shame. It would be five years before I would see him again.

During the first part of those five years, he would write me telling me that he was making excellent progress. He would send me samples of his work. In one of his letters he said, "Most Bible translators begin with the book of Mark, but I decided to start with Genesis." (Some translators begin with the book of Proverbs, but Mark is usually the starting point because it is a short book.) He said, "When we have tribal meetings each year, the elders tell a story about an ancestor that built a great boat and saved our people when the world was covered with water. I thought they would like to know who their ancestor was." Since his tribe had no written history they kept their past alive by passing these stories down from generation to generation by word of mouth. Gboffua included in his letter a little picture of the ark with the story in English, and in his language. We enjoyed these tidbits so much.

We sent Gboffua's support check each month and things seemed to be going smoothly. Then the war came. Soon his letters did not come anymore, and he was cashing his checks on an irregular basis. I flew to Nigeria intending to go on into Liberia, but could not get there because the planes were not flying, and I was told that it might be two months before I could get a flight into Liberia. Before returning to the States, I left a year's supply of checks in the hands of Mark, our translator in Nigeria, asking him to take the checks to Gboffua as soon as he could get there. They had never met each other, but they were both Bible translators. Eventually Mark was able to go to Liberia. The two of them had a wonderful week or ten days together. He delivered the checks, and again they were being cashed on a regular basis.

Suddenly the checks were no longer being cashed, and no more mail was received from him. There was silence. The Gulf War was taking place. Our news media was taken up with that, and we could not hear much about Liberia. We knew, however, because of our interest there, that Liberia was having a lot of trouble. We grew deeply concerned as the months passed with no word from Gboffua. We really began to pray and seek the face of God. The months dragged on, and on and the war worsened. We had news of the guerillas spraying a church with gunfire on a Sunday morning. Over 300 people were killed.

I told this to a church in Dallas, and a black man jumped out of his seat and ran down the aisle crying, "It is true! It is true! My mother was in that congregation, and she died that Sunday morning." The battle was so fierce that they could not remove the bodies. About three months later someone doused the scene with kerosene, and set it on fire to kill the stench. Over 200,000 people were beheaded. We knew all this, and we knew that our man was in this situation. We did not know where he was or what was going on, but we kept saying, "He is smart. He is strong physically. He is a wise man. If anyone can survive, he can."

Sometime later, on my way to the airport to catch a flight to China, I stopped in San Francisco and called my office in California. The lady who manages that office said, "Pastor, I had the strangest phone call this morning. It was from a lady in Maryland. She is not on our mailing list. She is not in our computer anywhere, but she called me a few minutes ago and said that she is listening to a Christian radio station in rural Maryland, and they are interviewing a medical doctor who has just returned from Liberia. He said he took a medical team in the back way through Ivory Coast, and while he was there he met an American lady with two little girls. The lady said that her husband was a Bible translator, and that she and the girls had gotten lost and separated from her husband. They were stranded in the backside of Liberia, and they did not know where he was. The caller understood the medical doctor to say that if he had enough money he could have brought the woman and the little girls out, but the soldiers wanted a bribe so he had to leave them there."

The lady who called, whom we do not know to this day, said to my office manager, "I believe he is talking about your people." Somewhere she had picked up a prayer request, and had presence of mind to call California and give us this news. I told Esther, my office manager, "Whatever you do, find that doctor. I am on a plane to China, but I will contact you later." She did, and the doctor confirmed that it was Elaine and the two little girls. The doctor said there were some Christians in the neighboring country that would go get her if we could provide funds to pay their expenses. We raised the money and sent it.

Someone asked, "How do you know that we can trust these people?"

I said, "All I know is that there is hope, and I am not going to have it on my conscience that I did not do my best."

Those African Christians walked into that jungle, over two hundred miles, found Elaine and her daughters, rescued them, and brought them out. One of the little girls had tuberculosis, and they did not know if she could make that trek because she would have to walk a lot, but they got her out. We had airline tickets waiting for them, and they flew home to New York City. I could not go to New York to welcome Elaine, so I called her and told her that we were so glad to have her back home. I asked if she had heard anything from Gboffua. She said, "If he were alive, I know he would have called us." That was the first time anyone had said that he might be dead.

At this time the burden of prayer and intercession was weighing heavier and heavier on us, especially on Lovie. She would wake me up in the middle of the night and say, "I am not willing for Gboffua to die. He is too precious. He has a ministry and a work to do. Let us pray one more time." We would lie there in bed, hug each other, cry, and pray begging God to spare Gboffua.

The months dragged on, and the burden grew heavier. Then we received a message from the doctor who had helped us find Elaine and the little girls. He said, "My friends in Ivory Coast, the Christians that rescued Elaine, have volunteered to go back to see if they can find Gboffua, and rescue him, if he is still alive, but they need money for the trip."

We raised more money. I called some pastor friends and they chipped in and we raised the money for this second rescue attempt. These African Christians again faced war and went into Liberia. For perhaps a month or two, we did not hear anything. Then one day we got a message, "Gboffua has been sighted!" What kind of message is that? At least it meant that he was alive! A week later we got another message, "Gboffua is a prisoner of war." We understood that to mean that he was alive and being held against his will. Then silence. Another week passed, and this short terse message came, "Gboffua has escaped!" Then dead silence for a month.

In the meantime, I knew that if he had escaped he would need an airline ticket. I knew that he was not an American citizen, but he was married to an American. I knew that if he tried to travel without a passport he would be in trouble. So, I called my congressman. His secretary answered in her Texas drawl. I tried to explain to her who I was and what I wanted, but I was not sure she understood what I was saying. When I hung up the phone I expressed my doubts that we would hear from that office again. In about thirty minutes, the phone rang and it was the State Department in Washington, DC. The voice on the other end of the line said, "Congressman Hall's office called, and I have been assigned to help you get your people out of Liberia." The guy asked what he could do. I told him that our man was not an American, but married to one and that he worked with us and would need a passport, travel papers, and an airline ticket. By now I had a little game plan. I figured that Gboffua would go to the American Embassy. Sure enough he did, and when he got there the travel documents were waiting for him, including an airline ticket.

The first words we had from him after these thirty days of silence was a call from his wife telling us that he had called her. He had shown up at a refugee camp run by Catholic sisters. They allowed him to make a phone call to America. He called the home of his mother-in-law and asked if she had heard from Elaine and the girls. She said, "They are here!" They had a celebration on the phone. In about seven days, he was in New York City. His church there chartered buses taking the choir and the orchestra to the John F. Kennedy Airport, and when Gboffua stepped off that plane they blew the roof off. He weighed one hundred pounds and was wearing the same clothes he had been wearing when he was captured, and they were in shreds. His friends wrapped him in an overcoat to keep him warm and to hide his nakedness.

In a few days he was in our office in Dallas. None of our staff had ever met Gboffua. I arranged chairs in a circle putting him in the middle, and asked him to tell us what God had done for him. The first thing he said was, "I do not hate anyone. I know Jesus better than I ever knew him, and I love him more than I ever loved him." Then he shared with us this amazing story: He said, "When I was in captivity I was beaten every day. My ribs were broken. I did not have a bite of food the whole month of August. I drank dirty water and prayed that my stomach would not hurt. At first, I could not understand why Elaine and I had gotten separated, but then I saw soldiers rape the women that were in the prison, and when the women became pregnant I saw the soldiers rip them open and pull out the fetuses laughing at the women as they died. Then I knew that if Elaine had seen that she would have gone mad. I knew then that it was the mercy of God that had allowed us to be separated. Only God sustained me."

I asked how he had escaped. He said, "Soldiers executed people every day, just for the fun of it. One morning they lined up thirty men; I was one of the thirty. These two big, burly soldiers came down the line cutting off heads with big machetes amid screaming, gore, and blood. As they neared where I was standing I said to God, 'I am ready to die, but I did not come here to die like this. I came here to write a Bible for my people, but I am going to die very shortly if you do not intervene.' The head of the guy standing next to me was severed, and just as this happened, the executioners got into a fight with each other. While they were trying to kill each other, I stepped backward into the bushes. When the fight was over they came back and continued their killing. They never missed me. I stayed hidden in the bushes all day. When night came, I started running. I would hide during the day and run at night, until I reached the border. Here I am; a testimony that God is faithful."

He said to me, "I lost my house, my vehicle, my computer, everything, and I lost five years of my work. It is all gone." He said, "Pastor, if you will get me a computer, I will start over before I forget much of what I had done. I do not want to lose what I did during the past five years."

Suddenly a light went on in my head, and I said, "Gboffua, is there any chance that you might have sent a set of your computer disks containing your work to anyone, anywhere, at anytime?"

He said, "Oh, I had completely forgotten about the Lutheran missionary that I met. He evacuated when the war broke out, and after he left I mailed him a set of my disks and asked him to help me with a problem I was experiencing."

I asked where he was, and he replied that he thought he was in Florida. I said, "Go into my office, get on the phone, and do not stop until you have found that guy."

About two hours later he came out grinning from ear to ear. He said, "I found him, and he has all of my computer disks and all of my work!"

The reason all that is fresh on my mind is because this week Gboffua heads back. He is going to Ghana to wait there for the fighting to die down and then go back into Liberia. I said, "Don't get caught. I do not know if we have enough faith to pray you out of there again." The point of the whole story is to talk to you about a God that answers intercessory prayer, about a God that does not abandon his people, about a God that can give a man grace. God's grace is sufficient."

Editor's note:

> As I worked on this manuscript in September 2013, I received word that Elaine Gboffua had died. May God's peace be with this family who has suffered so much for the cause of Christ.

A Sense of Destiny

Sitting in my office one day as a young pastor at a new church, suddenly I knew that God wanted me to lead that church in a mission's emphasis. Every church ought to have a sense of destiny. One reason churches have a lot of trouble and strife is because they have no sense of destiny. They have no high calling, no central purpose. One of the roles of a pastor is to lead the flock into greater things for God. It is his role to lead them beyond the four walls of the church and beyond the local community. Unless a church has a sense of destiny, it will always wallow in its own selfishness. I knew as I sat in my office that day that God wanted me to chart the course for that church. First of all to discern its destiny and declare it, then to provide the leadership to move that church forward to realize its destiny. I just said a mouthful, and I hope you heard what I said. If your church does not have that sense of destiny, your first assignment is to discern what the destiny of that church is in the economy of God and then cast the vision and provide the leadership and management to get your church moving toward that eternal destiny and divine assignment.

I was trying to discern what the destiny of the church was to be. I knew that God wanted to make it a great missionary church. I was a member of the Assemblies of God then. The organization was having its national convention in Long Beach, California, and I knew that people from all over the world would be coming. I had the bright idea that if I could get a national from Africa that had been saved as a result of missionary effort and stand him up in my church and say to my people, "This man is a trophy of God's grace and what your dollars and your prayers have done," it would be a real treat for the members of my church and somewhat of a shock treatment for them.

I called the Missions' Department in Springfield and asked who was coming to the convention. Brother Phil Hogan was the missions' director, and I talked with him. He called me several times asking me to let a buddy of his from England preach in my church. I told him that I did not want a white man, and I did not want someone from England. I told him that what my people needed to see was someone from Africa or India that had been saved because a missionary had gone there and preached the gospel. This sounds very common now, but it was not then.

Finally Brother Hogan told me about a little guy from Sri Lanka whom he thought was in Michigan at that time. He said, "I have not heard him preach. I do not know anything about him, but I have heard that he is quite fiery."

I hung up the phone and said to my secretary, "There is a little guy from Sri Lanka in Michigan. I want you to find him." She did the detective work and found the little guy. I invited him to come to the church and preach.

I later began to have second thoughts about my decision. I was a new pastor and wanted to make a good impression. I had invited to my church a man that I had never seen or heard anything about. I thought, *What if he cannot preach?* I have suffered great tribulation sitting on the platform while some turkey I invited into my pulpit dismantled my church. That is tribulation! The second half of the tribulation is suffered while I am sitting on the platform with a message waiting for my turn to preach and finally getting to the pulpit with eight minutes to deliver my sermon. You can go through the tribulation if you want, but I have been there twice already, and I am not going again. I began to have this, "Oh God, what have I done?" feeling. *What if he cannot preach? What if he drops the ball and there is egg on my face?*

So, to save my hide and to put in a little preventive maintenance, I invited Brother Edgar Bethany, a great man of God, to speak also. I asked Brother Bethany to preach about twenty minutes, and I asked the young guy to preach about twenty minutes. Many of my friends across the country had thought I was crazy to move to California. Some were coming for a visit for the first time and I wanted to have a good service.

It has been many years since that day, and when I go back to southern California people still ask me, "Where is the little fellow that preached that Sunday morning?" He got in the pulpit and pulled heaven down. It was as if lightening had struck the place. Incredible! While he was talking, he told about how he had grown up. He was a preacher's son. His daddy died while he was in Bible school. He had no clothes to wear, not even a shirt. The bill for his tuition came due and he could not pay it. He went to the seashore to pray, and there he told God, "If I cannot go to school, I will work and give half of the money I earn so that another boy can go to school." He said, "I stayed at the seashore three days and nights and prayed that prayer. I went back to the school to gather up my few belongings and face the reality that I was not going to be trained for the ministry. When I walked onto the grounds, Brother Graves, President of the college, said, 'Colton, come to my office.' In his office he said, 'Colton, an envelope came today from a lady in Florida, and she sent exactly enough money to pay your bill.' The letter read, 'Dear Brother

Perkins, I was praying today and God told me that a boy from Sri Lanka needs his school bill paid. I cannot find Sri Lanka on the map, but there must be such a place or God would not have said it. Brother Perkins, you know more about the world than I do. Wherever this place is, there is a boy from there who needs his bill paid, so rush this money to him.' It got there the day the bill had to be paid." That little lady's sacrificial seed grew into an unbelievable, fruitful tree.

When we got into the car to go to lunch I said, "Colton, I am from Florida. I was born there and grew up there. Who was the lady?" He said, "Her name was Percorni." I asked where she lived. He replied, "I think the name of the town was Lynn Haven (near Panama City)."

I said, "I know that town, and I know that lady." He said, "I wish she had not died. I would love to thank her for paying my way through Bible school."

"Colton, she is not dead unless she has died in the last few weeks. Just before I moved to California I was in her home. She lives in a little shack. She puts a bucket under a leak in the roof rather than spend money to have the roof repaired, so that she can buy tracts and help young folks get through Bible school. Hundreds of people come to her little shack for prayer."

"Do you think she is still alive?"

I said, "Her pastor is here at this convention. I will find out."

When I asked her pastor he replied, "Oh yes, she is still alive, but she has arthritis and cannot hold a pen any longer to write. She is nearly blind and in a wheelchair. She is a precious old saint."

I said to her pastor, "If you want to blow the roof off your church, you bring this fellow down there and wheel her out from one side and bring him out from the other and let them meet. Let each tell his or her story, and you will blow the roof off your church." The pastor bought the idea.

Colton said to me, "Where is Florida?" I told him that it was 2500 miles east. I scraped around and got enough money to buy his ticket to Florida. His pastor did exactly what I had suggested. They had the most glorious service you can imagine. There she was, her body gnarled with painful arthritis. And there he was, full of life and anointing.

I found out that this young guy had a church back in his country that met in a horse stall with a dried manure floor. He had sixty people in attendance. As the years passed, he became a powerful leader in that part of the world. In fact, today out there he is considered among the local people as Cho's (the Korean pastor) equal. You do not hear of him like you do Cho, but in the Orient he holds that kind of prestige. In fact, a church in Singapore just gave him $450,000 to help finish his new church that seats 5,000. When they dedicated it they invited me to be there. Thousands of people attended the Saturday night service and the three services on Sunday morning. It was truly like something out of the book of Acts.

In the eighties, Colton sponsored a convention at his church. He invited church leaders from eighty nations—third world countries. They met in the civic auditorium in the capital city of the country. The communists from China had built the building, and this was the first meeting—a red-hot Pentecostal service—to be held in the building, an auditorium built by the Chinese communists in a communist nation. Man, did we ever have a celebration! We baptized that civic auditorium! Only a handful of outsiders were invited. My wife and I were among the few white people there.

Basically, the whole theme of this gathering was, "Thank you, missionary, for coming. You brought the gospel. The gospel has changed our lives. We are forever indebted to you. Now your sons will take the torch. Your sons will take the flag and move it forward. Do not worry if you cannot get into Vietnam. We can go there. Do not worry if you cannot go to Cambodia. We will go there. Do not think the work of God has died because Americans and Europeans are shut out."

This challenge was powerful day after day. The last day, this little guy who had worshiped in a horse stall with a dried manure floor, and did not even have a shirt on his back when I found him (he had just a coat with an artificial collar) preached a most powerful sermon. When he finished he challenged each one to lay his life on the line. He said, "We are not going to let the devil have Vietnam. We are not going to let the devil have Cambodia. We are not going to let the devil have Iraq and Iran. We can go there, and we will, even if it costs us our lives."

Something like a big screen came down slowly out of the ceiling and a projector flashed on the screen a declaration patterned after our Declaration of Independence. It was done in beautiful calligraphy and read: "Whereas, we, of the Third World have received the gospel of Jesus Christ, and the power of that gospel has changed our lives; and, Whereas, the missionary cannot go but we can go…." There must have been twenty trumpets playing on each side, and he was saying, "Will you come and sign this declaration, putting your life on the line that you will give your life to see that the gospel goes out?"

Hundreds of those Third World leaders came. My wife and I got into the line and worked our way to a big scroll placed on a huge table, and we signed it—a covenant that we would not give up and that we would take the world for Jesus. Three thousand delegates signed this covenant. Signing that declaration was a powerfully emotional experience for my wife and me as we remembered the lonely little guy that we had found years earlier. He was now a world-class leader, and we were glorying in the small part we had in his life.

As we stood there, I saw a little brown hand come out from behind the curtains, and it reached for me. He pulled me saying, "Come." My wife and I went behind the curtain and there was Colton and Susan, his wife. Tears were rolling down his cheeks as he said, "Pastor Phillips, if it were not for you and Sister Phillips, this would never have happened. I just could not let you go by without personally thanking you. I wanted this moment with you and your wife so that I could tell you how much I appreciate what you have done and your love for us down through the years."

Of course, that comment ministered to me, but it is awkward and humbling to receive an expression of such import. I said to him, "Colton, I do not think that Lovie and I are the ones you should be praising God for. I think we ought to give glory to God for old Sister Percorni, the old woman who paid your way through school. That is who we ought to really be praising God for." The four of us agreed that she was the person who set the stage for this marvelous meeting, and we all joined hands and praised God for an old lady who was long since in heaven. That was a wonderful and tearful experience.

A few weeks later I was back in Florida and back in Sister Percorni's church. By that time, the church was run down, the neighborhood had changed, and there were mostly old people in the church, but they wanted me to come and preach. I had been preaching in that church since I was eighteen years old. You better believe I told what I had seen with my eyes, and I told what Sister Percorni had done. A lot of tears were shed, and we had a sentimental journey as I rehearsed the whole story. The older women who loved her, along with all the church members were glorying in their memory of this precious prayer warrior.

After the service, an old woman came hobbling down the aisle and said to me, "Son, I want to tell you the rest of the story." She said, "The last two years of Sister Percorni's life she was helpless. I bathed her. I fed her every bite of food she ate. I put her to bed, and I got her up. She lost her mind and her memory. She could not even remember her own name. She could not remember her children's names, but every now and then she would have lucid moments and she would say, 'They tell me that I paid a boy's way through college, and he has become a great spiritual leader.' Then she would lapse back into a semi coma. The day she died she sprang back to life that morning, and all day she rehearsed how that when she prayed God put into her heart to send money to pay a boy's way through Bible school. She would say, 'I did not patch the leak on my roof. I put a bucket under the leak. I took the money and paid a boy's way through school, and they tell me that he is a great man of God.' Sister Perconi told me that over and over, and all day she repeated that testimony. The last words on her lips were, 'They tell me that I paid a boy's way through Bible school, and that he has become a great man of God.'"

What a way to go! She will be waiting for him. There will be another reunion.

Adventures

Lost in Peru

I was in Peru preaching to a group of 400 native Peruvian pastors who had gathered deep in the jungle. Some of them had traveled by boat for two weeks to get there, and it would take two weeks to return home. Only one of those men could read and write. They had seen white men that were drug dealers. They had seen mining engineers. They had seen outlaws, but they had seen only one missionary. This whole work had been developed under the leadership of a Peruvian Indian pastor whose daughter was a member of my congregation in California. God supernaturally, over twenty years, brought me into a relationship with that Indian pastor, who, at the age of fifty, had lost his wife. Now his church had voted him out.

The missionary not only brought the gospel, he brought American church politics. Standing in front of a little church deep in the heart of the jungle, was this seventy-six-year-old man with an arm missing. I learned that his arm had been torn off when a horse ran away with him. He had not had medical care, so he had just a ragged nub. He stood there with tears streaming down his cheeks saying, "Brother Phillips, for a thousand miles down this river I have 125 churches that I have dug out of the raw with my bare hands. I have never had a car. I have walked. I have ridden a mule. I have lived on these boats, and every one of these people has been saved directly or indirectly under my ministry. I am going to be called to heaven soon, but I cannot live like this. I have slept on the ground and eaten monkey meat. I came to these jungles when I was fifty years old. I came to these jungles because I had a choice: I could be disillusioned and bitter or I could go do what God had been telling me in my heart for so many years. He had been saying, 'Go to the jungles. Go to the jungles. Go to the jungles.' Thank God I came here. Even if I did come with a broken heart, I took what was left of my life, and I have not been out of these jungles since I came. Brother Phillips, help me stabilize this work. Help me teach my preachers." That is why I was there. I was there to try to help. God put me there for a purpose.

We had a wonderful time as we met in those jungles. In one of the sessions, they chose their leader for the zone we were in—about forty churches. As they were installing their leaders, this tall, thin, young Indian man stood to make his acceptance speech. He said, "I am not worthy to serve you because my wife and I have been married nine years, and we have eight children. We do not know what causes children. We do not know where they come from. We pray to God that we will not have any more children. We love our children and we thank God for everyone of them, but we pray that we will not have any more." He continued, "The reason I am not worthy to be your leader is that I cannot feed my children. Since our children have come into the world, my wife and I have gone to sleep at night over the cries of our babies. They cry because they are hungry. It is not right for me not to be able to feed my family, so I am not worthy to be your leader." The other pastors were in the same situation, so they drafted him anyway. Something inside me hurt, and that is when we began to change the direction of what our organization would do for children of ministers and leaders.

I had hired a plane to take me into the area. The owners of the plane refused to bring me out until I could give them $800. It was a racket that I knew nothing about. I had walked right straight into it. That is the way the people who owned the planes dealt with the drug dealers, and they were used to the drug dealers having big rolls of bills. I had flown 17,500 feet over those mountains, dropped down into a valley on a dirt strip by a riverbank, and I was told, "You will never get out unless we take you out, and we are not going to take you out until you give us $800." I had no way of getting in touch with my wife. I was safe, but she did not know it because she had gotten a call from South Africa that the plane had been met and I was not on it. She said, "The last time I heard from him he was in the jungles of Peru." She was quite troubled.

Finally, the Indian brothers put me in a little Toyota that did not have a muffler on it. An Indian woman got under the wheel, and a mechanic got into the back seat with a toolbox, and they said, "We are going to take you out." It took us eleven hours to drive 125 miles at altitudes of 17,500 feet. We did not see another car all day. We saw big trucks hauling coffee and bananas. When that vehicle would bog down or get stranded on rocks, the Indians would get it out of the mud or over the rocks and tell me to sit still. When I got to the hotel room and called my wife, I was supposed to have been in Africa. She was glad to hear that I was alive. So, instead of continuing my trip, I just went home.

Four days later, I went to Dallas on business and to visit with our son who was in school there. The pain I was having in my body was incredible. I tried to get back on the plane but did not make it. That night I was admitted to the hospital, and eight doctors fought for a week to save my life. I had gotten some kind of jungle rot. They still do not know what it was. I was as green as a gourd.

When my wife finally got there from California, I had hoses, wires, pipes, and pumps attached to me and eight jungle-disease specialists hovering over me. The doctor said to me, "You are a strong man, and there is no need for us to play games with you; you are in big trouble. We do not know what is wrong with you, and we do not know how to treat you. We want to prepare you for any eventually."

The White Coat

I was invited to central Russia to speak at a ministers' conference for several hundred Russian pastors. A few years earlier I had had a very serious heart attack and a near death experience, but God had marvelously raised me up. Then I discovered that I was diabetic. Because of these health problems I had lost about thirty-five pounds, and had no intention of putting the weight back on. As you can imagine, my suit size changed, and I had a closet full of suits that were too big for me. I did not want to throw the suits away and I did not want to take them to Goodwill or the Salvation Army. They were suits for preachers, not homeless men. I thought about taking them to India but knew that if they were too large for me they would be much too large for an Indian brother. I knew they would be too hot for the preachers in Africa so I wondered, *Where am I going to take these suits?* I wanted preachers to have them.

When I received the invitation to go to Russia I knew what I would do with them. Many Russian men are about my size, so I bought a big, ugly suitcase and started packing my suits. It was quite an emotional experience as I began taking them off the clothes hangers and remembering where I had preached wearing them and how I had found this one and that one on sale, etc. It was kind of like giving your clothes away before you die instead of someone giving them away after you die.

While I was packing these suits, my wife, Lovie, came into the room holding a full length, white alpaca coat. If you did not know the difference you would think it was gorgeous white fur. I had bought that coat for her ten years earlier in Peru. We had a major Bible translation project among the Indians in the mountains of Peru, and on one of my trips there I saw the women of the tribe making these coats. I bought the coat for a ridiculously low price and brought it home to Lovie. It fit her perfectly. She looked like a model in it. It was my special gift to her, and I grinned and enjoyed seeing my lovely wife in this beautiful coat. We live in Texas, and in the area where we live the weather does not get very cold. The coat was designed for Eskimos, therefore my wife could only wear it perhaps two or three times a year. Two or three years had passed since she had worn the coat. I had not thought of the coat, but my wife came into the room holding it and said, "I feel that God would have me send this coat to a Russian pastor's wife." I thought this was a wonderful gesture, and I packed the coat with my suits and off to Russia I went.

When I arrived at the preachers' meeting, I said to the American missionary's wife, "I brought these clothes but I do not want to embarrass anyone, so I am going to leave this suitcase with you, and when I am gone you can distribute the clothes. You know the preachers and their clothing needs better than I. Please take care of this and distribute the suits as you see fit.

Being a typical preacher's wife she wanted to see what was in the suitcase. We opened it and there on the top was this gorgeous white coat. I mentioned that my wife had sent the coat for a Russian pastor's wife. Noticing that she was about my wife's size, I said to her, "Try it on." She did and I saw a sparkle in her eye. I encouraged her to take the coat, but she refused saying, "No. Your wife sent it to a Russian pastor's wife, and I could never take it."

Every day we had this conversation, but she continued to refuse. A couple of days before I was to leave I opened the subject with her again. I said, "I have heard you and your husband talking about being here only about two or three more years. Why don't you take the coat and wear it while you are here? When you leave you can give it to a Russian pastor's wife. The coat will bless you now and then it will bless the wife of a Russian pastor." I knew that the coat would last many years. She was persuaded and put on the coat. She looked super in the coat, and I could see the warm glow on her face.

The morning I left, this missionary's wife and her husband came to say goodbye. She said, "Before you go I want to share the rest of the story about the coat." She began, "Last winter I almost froze. We have been here several years, and my coat has worn very thin. The temperature reaches thirty to thirty-five degrees below zero and my coat is not adequate for the extremely cold weather. I would be chilled to the bone. Our budget is very limited and would not cover the purchase of a new coat for me. So, all last winter I prayed for a warm coat. This spring and into the summer I would say, 'God, I cannot face another Russian winter without a warm coat. Will you please give me a warm coat?' I never dream, but a few weeks ago I dreamed that someone gave me a full length, white fur coat. That dream was so vivid that I took it as an indication that God was going to answer my prayer. At breakfast the morning after the dream I told my family about my dream. My teenagers have teased me every day since I told them about my dream. They say, 'Well, has Joseph gotten her coat yet?' 'Where is your coat, mom?' 'Are you sure you did not eat a Russian hamburger before you went to bed?' They have been unmerciful in their teasing about my dream, but I wish you could have seen the faces of my three teenagers when I came downstairs this morning in this white coat. I had to practically pick them up off the floor. They were knocked out."

It took a while for all that to percolate in my spirit and for me to realize what God had done. God had anticipated a precious missionary's prayer for a warm coat ten years in advance. He had me buy it, not knowing what I was doing, thinking that I was going to bless my wife. My wife accepted it from me as a token of my love. That was all we knew. But in the economy of God, he foresaw, foreknew, and performed a miracle to put it in my heart in the mountains of Peru to buy a coat and take it all the way to Russia so that a missionary's wife would not be chilled to the bone in a Russian winter.

I did not fast and pray about that. I did not get a command from God. God used me like a donkey to be the delivery boy. I was a partner with God in taking a coat to a lady who had prayed it down out of heaven. There is a God in heaven, and that God does choose us to work with him to get his work done. Remember, "… for your Father knoweth what things ye have need of, before ye ask him" (Matthew 6:8).

True Dedication

Ministering to God

Many years ago, our church was involved in establishing and maintaining a leper colony in Liberia. Hundreds of lepers lived there, and our church was their main source of support. We had three or four missionary families ministering and working there. They had a hospital and a school. Many Americans visited that leper colony. One day, a typical, ugly American tourist with his bright sport shirt, shorts, camera, and all the paraphernalia came. A little nurse was bent over a black man's foot that was half rotted off with leprosy, picking out the dead flesh and the putrid corruption and infection, trying to bring some relief to this suffering man who was dying with leprosy.

This American tourist was watching her over her shoulder. He gagged a couple of times and said, "I would not do that for all the money in the world."

The little nurse, casting a glance toward him said, "Neither would I, mister. Neither would I."

At some point there has to come a change in our life to where we understand that the person we are really responding to is God, and we are ministering to God's needs not human needs.

Tonight in Ghana one of our missionaries is living in a village in a very primitive situation where a thousand people have been killed and over a thousand houses burned. She is an orthopedic surgeon. She could have made $200,000 last year in an orthopedic hospital in Memphis where she had a practice, but she is out there where there is no air-conditioning, where there is hell and war and dirt and blood and mud, but those skilled hands are making little children walk. But making little children walk will not keep her there. The only thing that will keep Dr. Jean Young in that village is for her to get away from those children and away from the gore and demands and get quiet before God and hear one more time that it is to him she is ministering. It is to him that she brings cold water, and it is to him that she offers her life. "In as much as you have done it unto one of the least of these…you have done it unto me" (Matthew 25:40).

Focus on Something

The pastor of a great church in Birmingham, Alabama, is on the board of directors at Evangel Bible Translators, and is a longtime personal friend. They have been through exactly what many of you are going through. One day Bob said to me, "Tell me what is on your heart. What are you praying about?"

I said, "Bob, I sit at my desk, and every time I open mail I find perhaps a hundred letters of urgent appeal—good legitimate causes. I read thousands of these letters in the course of a year. My phone rings, 'Brother Syvelle, can you help us? We need to build a building for orphans. We have a church that needs a roof. We have preachers who are hungry and children who are starving.' All day every day this goes on." I said, "There is one letter that I cannot shake. I have been told that there are fifty five million Muslims in central Russia that need a Bible. They have never had a Bible. They do not speak Russian. They suffer under the double curse of communism and Islam. They have never had the Word of God and have never had a chance. I would like so much to give those people the scripture.

"The amazing thing is that I have a couple that I can send immediately. They have completed their training and can go immediately to begin that project. I am tired and weary. I do not have it in me to tour this country begging churches to support that project. I said to God, 'Father, I really feel this ought to be done. I have been quickened by the need, but I don't have the energy or the will to tour this country begging a hundred churches to support that project.' I told him that if he wanted it done, he would have to give me the resources to fund the project in ninety days, and that if it did not come in ninety days, I couldn't do it."

My friend looked at me very thoughtfully. That night he stood up in his church and said, "Folks, for years we have prayed that God would give us something special as a church that we could do that would have a significant impact on the world." He told them about our conversation. I never once thought about his being the source. We were just close friends.

He said to me, "That is one project you do not have to worry about. Our church is going to take that project, and we are going to give fifty-five million people the Word of God in their language."

I said, "But, pastor, do you understand that I am talking about twenty years?"

He said, "I understand."

Every month that church funds that project. When it is all over they will be the congregation that has the joy of knowing what they have done. That kind of commitment puts power and dignity into the project. That has been the easiest project we have ever managed because we know that the funds are there. We know the prayer is there. That church has something that is theirs, something that is significant. "Ask and it shall be given unto you" (Matthew 7:7).

Going to Goeno

Editor's note:

This story is so big and powerful that it had to be placed in a chapter of its own. This is one of the clearest pictures of missionary work that you will ever experience.

Instead of taking a passage of scripture and dealing with it like I normally do, I want to tell you about a trip that I made to New Guinea many years ago. As I share this story, I want you to hear, loudly and clearly, this truth: If God puts a dream in your heart, if God speaks to you, if God calls you, if God leads you, if God deals with you, it might take a long time for what God has spoken to you by the Spirit to come to pass, but it will come to pass. We get distracted by what some of our brethren have done or failed to do. I think it is about time that we lift up our eyes and see that while God's heart has been broken, he has not withdrawn to some corner to nurse his wounds. He is alive and well, and he is active in this world, and great and mighty things are happening, for which we can praise God.

On a Sunday morning, I was speaking for the first time in a new church just north of San Francisco. Into that service walked a young couple who had never been to that church. After the service they came to me and introduced themselves as missionaries to New Guinea, and they asked if my wife and I could have lunch with them. Along with the pastor, we arranged to take this couple out to eat and spend some time with them. During the course of our visit, we learned that they had served the Lord as missionaries in New Guinea for four years. They shared with us how this came about.

Years earlier, they had met a veteran missionary who had been in New Guinea many years. He lived across the mountains several hundred miles from where the young couple now lived. This old veteran missionary had learned that he had cancer and less than a year to live, if God did not see fit to heal him. He had lived a long and fruitful life and felt that his time to die had come. However, his concern was for someone to take his place. So, he asked Mike and Barbara to prayerfully consider taking over his mission station. The mission station consisted of a Bible school, twenty-two churches, seventy preaching points (places where they held services on a regular basis with no church building), and a hospital clinic. This was a well-established mission that needed new leadership to carry on the work after the old missionary's death.

Mike and Barbara approached their denomination for approval and blessing on this new venture. The organization's leadership saw only problems, and they did not want anything to do with it. They eventually told Mike and Barbara that if they insisted on assuming this responsibility, which, in their opinion, was far too much for them, the denomination would ask them to resign from its membership. Mike and Barbara did resign, because they felt that God had spoken to them, and was leading them into this new work. They began making preparations to go to New Guinea. In due time, Evangel Bible Translators had a part in helping this couple get back to New Guinea. Our organization provided a motorcycle and several other things to help them.

After their return to New Guinea, Mike wrote me a letter asking me to come to New Guinea to speak at his annual ministers' conference and camp meeting. He was deeply concerned that the people to whom he ministered had no scriptures in their language, because their language had never been written. He wanted me not only to speak but also to consider and investigate starting a project to write a Bible for these people.

So, I went to Australia and on to New Guinea. My son, Darin accompanied me. I used some of my frequent flier miles to get him a free ticket to go with me.

In Australia, we boarded a small plane and flew about three hours up to New Guinea, and then on a smaller plane we flew up to a little town in the mountains called Garoka. There are no roads to Garoka; you have to fly to get there. The American military built a landing field there during the war. Mike met us in Garoka, and in his four-wheel drive vehicle we traveled another four hours up the mountain to his mission station.

Mike has red hair and a big, red beard and looks like an outdoorsman extraordinaire. He was very glad that we had come, and he was so excited about the upcoming meeting. And as we started the long ride to reach our destination, Mike began to tell us the story of what he had learned about this mission station and the missionary who had established it. It took the whole four hours to tell the story. Of course, on the way we passed a few fellows with bows and arrows and spears, but that did not bother Mike. He was praising the Lord for sending him to such a beautiful place to do God's work.

On the way from the airport to the mission station, Darin was sitting in the front seat, and I in the back. About thirty minutes up the mountain, Darin looked back and grinned at me and said, "Daddy, I think we have found a real missionary."

Every now and then you meet somebody who has a touch of God upon him, is full of the joy of the Lord, and happy to be in the vineyard doing God's will. Mike was like that. With his red beard flapping and his hair blowing in the breeze as he drove up the mountain, Mike told about this fellow, Ben, who established the mission station.

During World War II, Ben was in a battle with the Japanese, and it looked like everyone would be killed. They were down in the South Pacific in one of those out-of-the-way forgotten places where thousands of Americans and Japanese died and are buried, and for all practical purposes forgotten. Ben told God that if he would let him live, he would be a missionary and come back to that place and preach the message of God's love. God spared him, and he never gave up on that idea. He did not make a promise and then forget it. He spent several years getting ready to go back down there as a missionary. All this time he was praying, "God, where should I go?" Every time he would pray, he would hear one word deep in his spirit "Goeno." After some time he decided that Goeno was the name of a place, and eventually he decided that that was where God wanted him to go. He searched high and low, on every map, in every Atlas. He checked with all the governments, but nobody had ever heard of a place named Goeno. Finally, he became convinced that Goeno was in New Guinea and that it was his responsibility to find this place. He took his wife and baby girl and went to New Guinea, and there they began to search for Goeno. They went everywhere they could go by road. Nobody there had ever heard of the place.

Many months later, traveling high in the mountains in a rugged and wild area, he pitched his tent by a river, and from that base camp he would make scouting trips looking for Goeno. One day a New Guinea warrior, a man who was ninety percent naked, with a bow and arrow came into the camp. By now, Ben was able to converse in the native language well enough to communicate.

He asked this fellow if he knew of a place named Goeno. The warrior's face lit up, and he said, "That is where I live." Ben asked where it was located, and the warrior told him that he could reach Goeno in two weeks by foot. He said, "You come and see Goeno. Goeno nice place. You like Goeno; you live in Goeno."

So, Ben decided that he had better talk to the Australian Magistrate, since at that time New Guinea was under the jurisdictional control of Australia. It took Ben several weeks to reach Port Moresby by foot. When he told the Magistrate that he was looking for a village named Goeno, the Magistrate said, "There is no such place." By now Ben had been able to locate the general area on the map, but the Magistrate told him that no soldiers or anyone else had ever been into that area, because it was wild territory, and that Ben could not go there. Ben told him that he believed God was telling him to go, and he planned to obey God. The Magistrate said, "I cannot forbid you to go, but if you intend to go, you will have to pay me a $750 deposit in case you get killed. That will pay for retrieving your body."

Right about here is where we separate the missionaries from the would-be missionaries. In our organization, we have all the missionaries come in and spend about three days with us before they go overseas. This is the final stop before they depart America. They have to make a will and do all kinds of paperwork. Included in the final paperwork is a form they must sign giving us instructions about what to do with their bodies in case they are killed. Some of them turn green and stutter a bit at this point, but these are the requirements. Our organization has to guarantee the government that we will take care of the missionaries and retrieve their bodies if they are killed. So, I understand the Magistrate's demand for a deposit. You know the great commission never says anything about coming home anyway. It just says, "Go!" There is no closed country if you are not worried about coming home. That coming home part is what defeats so many people. It is the "go ye" that we ought to be concerned about.

So, poor Ben had to come up with a $750 deposit. This done, he started the return trip to the base camp where he had left his wife and child. When he reached the campsite, his tent was gone and so were his wife and baby. Everything was gone. The ground was clean. Of course, you can imagine the shock and panic Ben felt. Shortly, someone found him and tried to make him understand that the warrior who had come several weeks before had reappeared with 200 warriors taking his wife, his baby, and his tent to Goeno. He learned that it had taken those soldiers almost a month to get his wife and child and their belongings to Goeno. Ben was told not to worry about his family; they were being cared for. It took Ben almost a month to get to Goeno. When he finally arrived in this native town high in the mountains, the warriors had set up his tent and had begun building a house for him and his family.

He discovered that thousands of people lived across those mountains and he knew that he was where God had told him to go so many years before. He built a house, a church, a clinic, and a complete mission station. At one point he brought a small, portable, lightweight sawmill up there to cut timber for the buildings. Ben had a vehicle down at the coast, and since there were no roads it took 1,000 men ten months to go to the coast and get his car and bring it to Goeno. I stood in Goeno and looked down a steep incline to the raging river 3500 feet below where I was standing. (*National Geographics Magazine* just had a helicopter in there taking pictures of that raging river.) Those natives brought Ben's car across that ravine and one hundred other ravines like that. They used ropes made out of vines to move the vehicle over this treacherous and wild terrain, and it took them ten months to complete the project. I talked to some of those men just a few weeks ago.

Ben wanted his vehicle up there because there was no road and he wanted to build one starting in Goeno and going back out to the government station. They had no tools with which to do survey work. They would get the vehicle up there and let it roll back and judge how steep the grade was, etc. They had no axes, no shovels, no hoes. They worked over ten years to build a fifteen-mile stretch of road with sticks. In 1953, the people of Goeno had never seen an ax or a blade. They were a Stone Age civilization. We do not think they had ever seen a wheel until Ben came. He preached seven years before the first person was saved.

The situation began to change with an eclipse of the sun. The sun went dark in the middle of the day scaring the daylights out of those natives. Ben had been telling them about a God in heaven. Of course, they had no concept of a God in heaven. The only gods they knew were bad spirits in the trees, in the ground, and in the graves. When the eclipse happened, hundreds of them came running to him asking him to pray that the God he had been talking about who lived up in heaven would be merciful to them. These were his first converts. Some of those fellows who got saved that day are pastors now. Praise God, the work began to grow.

So, when we got to Goeno we saw all of these nice buildings—hospital, Bible school with twenty boys studying for the ministry, a church that seats several hundred, and a tent. The tent was there for our meeting. They were expecting 1,000 people to attend the meeting, but on the first night attendance was over 1,500. There were no chairs; people were sitting on the ground with legs crossed. The weather was cold and damp because of the elevation (7,500 feet), but they were ready to have church. There were three language groups represented at the meeting, and this was the first time these groups had ever worshipped together. After having fought each other for thousands of years, they stacked their bows and arrows and came under that tent, and together they sang the praises of God day and night! Many of you have heard of a language called pidgin English. It is a language that evolved out in the South Pacific to help people who do not speak each other's language to communicate, particularly for trade, etc. At the services, an interpreter standing beside me translated my English into pidgin (a blend of two languages), and then from pidgin to the next language, and from that language to the next. So, everything I said had to be translated three times.

To give you an idea about how this all went. Here I was a tall, oversized, white man. Another white man introduced me. Then a small black man came to stand beside me. He spoke excellent English, so he could understand what I was saying. Now, there is enough English in the pidgin English that I could understand some of the words. My introduction was translated like this: "He be big man. He come on big bird from far, far away. He be speaking loud for Papa God forty-one Christmases" (meaning I had been preaching loudly for Father God forty-one years). They do not count time in years, but Christmases. That was how my introduction started. When they sing "How Great Thou Art," they sing, "He big fella; he fine fella; he live on high; he Papa God; he number one." I like that, don't you? God is a fine fellow; he is number one. Praise God! And he big fella, too. Amen! We had a marvelous time, day after day, service after service.

While there, I learned that these people had a tremendous fear of death, particularly before they became Christians. They lived in the fear that witch doctors would put curses and hexes on them and cast spells on them causing them much pain and suffering; that is the only life they had ever known. These people are just a step from the Stone Age, today. In fact, the only man on that mountain who drives a car is Mike. I am going to try to get someone to teach those native boys how to drive a truck so they can help Mike with some of the driving. They have twenty guys in Bible school learning to preach. Churches are the same the world over. Let me just give you a little insight.

A delegation of these native people who are still nearly in the Stone Age showed up at the convention. They were having big trouble in their little church over the mountain, and they wanted a new pastor—just like in America. When asked what the problem was they said, "We love our pastor; we appreciate him, but we are tired of him. He is old, and his memory is bad; we have heard him preach the same thing until we cannot stand it any longer." The pastor cannot read or write and does not have any scripture in his language. The training he had received in the little Bible school taught him to tell Bible stories using a flip chart. On one page of the chart would be a picture of Moses, on another page Elijah, on another page Jesus, on another Paul, on another the birth of Jesus, and on another the resurrection. They had thirty of these pictures on a flip chart, and that is what they were taught in Bible school. They would go out into the villages and tell a story connected with the picture. So, for all of these years that old pastor, who cannot read or write, and had nothing written in his language, would tell stories. This delegation of primitive people told us that they were sick and tired of these stories. They had heard them until they knew them by heart. They wanted a young preacher with fresh new messages. We had to referee all of that while we were there.

At the clinic (they call it the sick house), Mike's wife, an expert nurse, sees 150 patients a day. With two native helpers, she delivers babies and does minor surgeries. The helpers are able to give shots, bind up wounds, etc. The ministry that Mike and Barbara have is quite amazing. They are training twenty boys for the ministry, still using the flip chart because they have nothing to read. One of the missionaries had carried a television and a VCR up to the village. They have a big diesel generator that produces electricity for a couple of hours each night. The missionaries had a special video film that they wanted all the natives to see. Of course, the natives wanted to see the television because they had never seen one. Only the men were allowed to see the film, because of the subject matter—wife beating. Wife beating was a common practice in the villages. Because of the large number of men, a system for viewing the video was devised so that nobody would see it twice (different colored slips of paper were drawn for each viewing—one for Monday night, another for Tuesday night, etc.) The film had been produced in New Guinea by a missions' organization to deal with the universal problem of wife beating.

The missionaries told me that there was not a man in those mountains that did not beat his wife on a regular basis. In fact, an Assemblies of God missionary told me that he was down there preaching, and did not know anything about all of the wife beating when suddenly during the sermon he said, "I just feel in my spirit that someone in this church has been beating his wife, and it is wrong! You ought to repent! Come up here, and I am going to lay hands on you and pray for God to forgive you." He said that every man in the church came forward including the pastor.

The gospel is about confronting a culture that is out of the will of God and confronting things that are wrong in the lives of people. I said to the fellow in charge, "It is wonderful that you are showing it to the men, but there are several hundred little boys here who need to see the film also, so that they, too, will understand that wife beating is wrong. Barbara, the nurse, said that not a day goes by that she does not patch up a woman's injuries— limbs or head—resulting from a beating by her husband. There is a cruelty in that culture, but Jesus came to change those cruel customs. I really preached about how Jesus elevated the position of women in society and how he gave women nobility and taught us to love and respect them. There is power in the gospel to change how people live.

The convention leaders wanted me to talk to all the ministers. My allotted time was one hour and twenty minutes—twenty minutes to give a devotional message and one hour to talk to the preachers. About one hundred preachers attended the meeting. They sat with legs crossed on the floor and most of them were two-thirds naked. Some were wearing used clothing that had been shipped to them. When the question and answer time came, an old gray-haired papa with a big, natural afro and a long, gray beard (the New Guinea men have long, pointed beards) was the first to ask a question. It was obvious that he was an elder among them and had probably been appointed to ask questions. This old, black papa raised his hand for recognition and said, "Tell me for true for true, I want to hear from your own lips what day of the week God want me to worship him. Before you white skins came we knew no God. You tell us that there is a great God in heaven with great power. Eventually we believe, and we come to love and serve him, and we want to please him. You tell us to worship God on Sunday. We know no Sunday. Before the white skins come we never hear of Sunday. We know no days of the week."

To this day, they do not know when they were born or how old they are. Time is measured by events, and to keep the story alive every year at this camp meeting they have a drama re-enacting the arrival of the missionary to their village. They want to keep the story alive for their children. They call him the great one. They re-enact the coming of the Great One. But that old man said to me, "We know no Sunday. We know no day until the white skins come, but when the white skins come and tell us about this great God in the heavens, they said worship God on Sunday, so we worship God on Sunday. Now," he said, "new white skins come and these new white skins say worship God on Saturday. We know no Saturday, but the new white skins say that if we do not worship God on Saturday he will be very angry. Now, sir, you tell me for true, do we worship God on Saturday or worship him on Sunday?"

I spent the next hour and a half trying to tell them why we worship God on Sunday and why we keep every day holy, and why, why, why. Even while I was talking God would give me new understanding and I would try to get on another subject, but they wanted to come right back to that subject, because they did not want the great God who lives in heaven to be angry with them. They wanted to please him. Then the old man said, "We no read the Book." His language had never been written. There was no scripture. He was telling us that we would have to read the Book and tell it to him, and he said, "Now you, sir, tell me for true what the Book says."

Brother, it will knock your socks off to know that you can read the Bible and he cannot. I must have twenty versions of it, and he does not even have John 3:16. That ought to make you think and make you know that what God has called us to do in Bible translation is not a joke. I was so deeply moved.

The next day, I met with the elders of the church. Now, these are people who were Stone Age men until 1953. We talked for long hours about their need for the Word of God in their own language. The thing that was eating at me was the fact that, if we could have started the next day to begin to write the New Testament in his language, that old papa who asked me those searching questions would be dead long before we could ever complete the copy. That thought haunted me.

The young man, David, who had interpreted for me was a New Guinea native, educated in Australia at the university, and spoke excellent English. He served as the governor's personal assistant. I said to David, "You read and understand English so well, and you fluently speak your mother tongue. If I gave you a copy of the New Testament, could you do a narration? Could you read your version of the story of the birth of Jesus, the miracles that Jesus performed, the death and resurrection of Jesus onto a cassette, a sentence at a time?" Now we are not going to pretend that this is a precise translation. He said that he could. I told him that we had the equipment, and could edit out every pause and every stop and could put it together so that it would flow smoothly with no pauses or clicks. Then I said, "We have a solar-powered cassette machine that would enable that old papa, who asked me those questions yesterday, to hear the Word of God in his own language. Could we do that?" That council of elders agreed that we should do that first, and then follow that with the written Word of God in their own language.

You thought I was going to start raising money to pay for all this, didn't you? Let me tell you something else. I told God that there was no way we could start that mission with all the other things we had going, and that he would have to do something special to help us. I had figured that it would cost a minimum of $10,000 just to get the equipment, and put everything in place to get started. The members of the first two churches where I shared this story stood and said, "We will pay the first $10,000." So, that must mean that God wants it done! Now, we are going to have to buy dozens, maybe hundreds, of these cassette machines for the people of Goeno to hear the Word of God. We want every church, every village there to hear.

The last night I preached in New Guinea, the tent was filled. Approximately 2000 people were there. They were sitting on the ground—packed in. By then I had picked up on their fear of death, their fear of the unknown, and their fear of the future. Fears were so close to the surface in the minds of those people who were just a step removed from pagan darkness. I tell you, God helped me to preach under a powerful anointing, and I preached that night on "Things Jesus Never Did." Among the things he never did was go to a funeral. He did not bury the dead; he raised the dead. He had something in him that would not let him participate in a funeral. He faced death and he conquered death. To emphasize that point I said, "You know, the lesson we need to learn is that the God we serve will not leave us buried in a hole in the ground. He is going to come again, and we are going to be raised from the dead. Death and the grave have no hold on us. Death has no sting and the grave has no victory!"

I could hear my interpreter speaking in pidgin English saying, "Papa God, he fine fellow. He not going to leave us in a hole in the ground. He coming from on high! He going to make us live again! Praise God! Death has no power over us. Papa God, I love you. I love you, Papa God!"

That audience exploded, standing to their feet, with their hands raised and tears streaming down their cheeks shouting, "Papa God, we love you! Papa God, you no leave us in the ground.

Papa God, you coming back for us. Papa God, you conquered death. Papa God, we love you! Praise God!"

Aren't you glad that we have this book to read? We do not have to depend upon someone else to read it to us. Aren't you glad that we know that Papa God does not care what day of the week we set aside for worship? Aren't you glad that Papa God is friendly and that he is not going to kill you somewhere or put a hex or a curse on you? He loves you! The only difference between them and us is about fifteen generations. Our forefathers were pagan just like they are, and the gospel has made the difference.

That is just an example of what God is doing. All over this world God is moving. How many of you will tell God that you want to be a part of what he is doing in the last days? I do not want to be left behind, do you? God, you are moving by your power; you are moving by your Spirit; you are working in the world, and we thank you that you have not abandoned planet earth. We thank you that you are still in the business of establishing your kingdom and making your name known. You are pushing back the darkness.

We were riding in the Jeep one day, when suddenly Mike slammed on the brake and said, "There he is! There he is!" It was an old man on a walking cane with a white beard, and Mike said, "That is the soldier that found Ben and told him about Goeno."

My son was able to film over one and a half hours of an interview with him. He told of finding Ben and bringing him to Goeno and of hearing the gospel. As we stood on a mountain about twenty miles from the mission station, Mike said, "Do you see that church over there (it was several miles away)?" We were high up in that mountain, the day was clear, and we had a great view. Mike said, "Look across the valley to where you see the smoke rising, we have a church there, and we have a preaching point beyond that peak over there." And then he turned and said, "Do you see that river and those mountains beyond the river? For 1,000 miles there is not a church, not a Christian. That is another language and another people, but God is going to help me train those twenty boys in Bible School, and we are going to climb that mountain, and we are going to swim that river, and we are going to make Jesus known there like he is known in Goeno. It is all about making Jesus known where he has never been known! "The Lord is…not willing that any should perish, but that all should come to repentance" (2 Peter 3:9).

The Holy Spirit Works

India

It is marvelous how the Holy Spirit works. I want to tell you about a visit to India by invitation from two tribes of people that live up on the border of China and Burma and Sikkim—way up north. We flew to the last airport and then rode in a four-wheel drive vehicle for five hours to get to where I was to preach.

In the early turn of the last century—1902–05—Baptist missionaries went into this area. The people were not Hindu. They were not Buddhist. They were Animists. They had no religion except the worship of their ancestors. They were pagans. When the gospel came, thousands of them turned to Christ. There was a church in every town and community, and some of them were large churches. Fifty years ago, a man was praying on the top of a mountain and

God marvelously, gloriously, and overwhelmingly baptized him in the Holy Ghost. His experience with God was so profound and powerful, his witness so alive with the things of God that in a matter of months hundreds of people had been baptized in the Holy Spirit and within a few years thousands of people. The original church turned thumbs down on this experience, and consequently many turned away from God. Now the big churches are empty, and people have gone back to their pagan ways on a large scale.

From the influence of this man, who had been baptized in the Holy Spirit, hundreds of Spirit-filled churches have sprung up. The miracle of this is that there have been no missionaries allowed in that area since before World War II. I had to get a special permit from the government to go in this time. There were fifty-year-old preachers at this celebration who had never seen a white man. There had been no outsiders in there at all. They built a tabernacle with bamboo poles, tied those poles together with ropes, cleared off a place on the top of the mountain where the man had received the Holy Spirit, called for a fiftieth-year celebration, and invited me to come and speak. What a privilege! The first man to receive the Holy Spirit sat on the platform while I preached. He was old, gnarled, twisted, and walked with a limp, but he was still alive, and the fire of God was still in his soul.

A delegation of twenty-two men walked out of Burma for two days to join the celebration. Another delegation of over twenty men walked out of Sikkim, a neighboring nation, and a group of eighteen men, former headhunters, from one of the tribes that we are working with to give them a Bible, walked barefoot for two days. One old fellow had two big holes in the lobe of his ear. In another meeting I had heard him praying, and he was punching holes in heaven. He was not a stranger at the throne. I could not understand a word that he was saying, but my spirit bore witness that he knew God and he knew how to pray.

I asked the fellow who works with us, and speaks English, to ask the old man to give his testimony. He stood and said, "When the gospel came to our tribe I did not believe. My friend was the first to receive the gospel and accept Christ. We persecuted him by hanging him and his wife upside down in a tree by their heels, not letting their hands touch the ground. We thought they would die if we left them there all night. We did that two times, but they did not die. We burned down their house four times, but they did not give up. When he built a little church, we burned it down, but he did not give up. I said to myself, 'I had better have a look at this Jesus that my friend has found.' Now I am saved and full of the Holy Ghost, and I am a preacher of the gospel." He had a bag on his side, and he said, "I used to carry men's heads in this bag, but now I carry the Word of God."

His tribe did not have a Bible. He had a Bible from another tribe. He could not read it, but he had a Bible. This man said, "When I used to cut off the head of an enemy, I would parade down the streets, strutting like a cock carrying the head of the man I had killed, and my people would applaud. At a ceremony holes would be punched in my ear—one hole for each man I had killed. I still have holes in my ear, but I do not cut off men's heads anymore. I get people saved and full of the Holy Ghost!"

There is power in this gospel! There are hundreds of churches, and no missionary. The computers say that these are unreached people. They have thousands and thousands of born again believers, and well-run churches with 400, 500, and 1,000 people in them. Computers do not always have accurate information. God gets ahead of computers. Someone feeds data, combing through statistics, and putting out all these reports. I am glad they do this work, but there is no computer in the world that can keep up with the Holy Spirit's work.

Eskimos

One of the sharpest and brightest couples that ever came to us desiring to be Bible translators said that God had put on their hearts a burden to translate a Bible for the Eskimos that live above the Arctic Circle in the Soviet Union. They said, "We have done our research. No missionary has ever been there. There is no church there and no gospel."

We were all enthused about helping them. They got their training and raised their support. We had a farewell service for them and off they went. We were so excited that we were going to reach people in that frozen part of the world that had never heard the gospel. In about two weeks I received a message: "We do not know what went wrong, but when we got here we found sixteen churches and several hundred believers, and someone has a New Testament half-translated. What are we going to do?"

I said, "Move on to someone else who needs you." That information did not show up in anyone's computer. The Holy Spirit is leaving tracks everywhere in this world, and we ought to celebrate the fact that his truth is marching on. There is victory in the name, "Jesus." There is power in the name, "Jesus." His glory is being revealed in the whole earth. "…all of the earth shall be filled with the glory of the Lord" (Numbers 14:21).

Pakistan

Three or four weeks ago, a man came to my office, introduced himself, and told me that he was born in Pakistan. He had European features and did not look like an Arab at all. He is part of a language group that has 14,000,000 people in it. They live in northern India, Pakistan, and Iraq. If you have ever been to India you likely noticed big trucks made by the Tata Company. The Tata Company is like General Motors. The company builds everything, but is famous for those huge, ugly trucks that you see all over India. This corporation has computer companies and banks. The Tata family is from this language group. Many leaders emerge from this language group. There are sports figures and heroes in India and Pakistan that are from this language group. He said, "Out of 14,000,000 people there are only twenty believers. No missionary has ever gone to my people. There is no gospel tract, no songbook, no scripture. Only twenty of us have ever found Jesus. I am a professor at a university in Maryland. I have three master's degrees. I have had some training to be a Bible translator. God has called me to write a Bible in my language."

He just needed help and encouragement, and during my visit with him he told me that his people had never seen even a gospel tract written in his language. Not one scrap of paper about Jesus had ever been produced for 14,000,000 people.

He said, "I have been praying, and God has given me, I believe, a revelation of what to write. King Cyrus in the Old Testament was from my language group. In my language group, when we talk about our ancestors King Cyrus is always remembered like Americans remember George Washington. In our language group when a father is teaching his son he will say to him, 'Do the righteous thing.' Righteousness is a big part of our culture, but we do not know how to obtain righteousness, because we have never had the gospel. What I have felt God would have me do is to write a pamphlet so that when I tell my people that Isaiah, the prophet, prophesied the birth of King Cyrus sixty years before he was born, I can also tell them that Isaiah prophesied the coming of another king whose name is Emmanuel. I want to tell them that if Isaiah was accurate in predicting the birth of one of our ancestors, who became a leader of notoriety, he was also accurate in prophesying the birth of the king whose name is Emmanuel. I want to help them understand that if Isaiah was right the first time then he was right the second time and we need to get acquainted with the second great king that the great prophet predicted would be born."

The Spirit of God came upon me while he was talking to me, and I knew that we needed to print about a ton of those tracts. He said, "My people will read the tracts because I will be telling them about their ancestor, one they know about. I am going to talk to them and challenge them that if they believe Isaiah was right the first time they must believe that he was right the second time, and that we need to have a look at the other great King. From there I will give them the plan of salvation."

"I will lead them in paths they have not know; I will make darkness light before them, and crooked things straight" (Isaiah 42:16).

God's Mysterious Ways

Little Things Become Big

When I pastored in California, some missionary friends introduced me to a little Mongolian barbeque restaurant, just a hole in the wall, owned by people from Mongolia who came across China, down to Formosa, and somehow got to the States bringing with them the strangest-looking stove you have ever seen. In time, they opened a little restaurant. They spoke no English, so there was no verbal communication between you and them. You would choose your food from a smorgasbord of vegetables, meats, seasonings, etc. It was then cooked and served to you on a bed of rice. Delicious! While I was waiting for my food one day, I noticed a placemat on the table. It had pictures on it of Mongolians riding ponies, a camel caravan, and two or three paragraphs telling about Mongolia, its geography, its people, and its location. The country is sandwiched between China and Russia in a remote part of the earth. Its inhabitants are nomads, and life there is harsh. That was about all I had ever read about Mongolia. Perhaps I had read a story about Mongolia in *National Geographic*, but I did not remember much about it.

As I sat in that little restaurant thinking about the family of Mongolians that had somehow come out of Mongolia, a land of several million people, lugging an old iron stove all the way from there to America to make a living, I wondered how many of the people in Mongolia had ever heard the name of Jesus. I did not know of a single missionary or a single Christian in that land. The missionaries that had gone there had either died or left in defeat. As far as I knew, there was not a church or a believer in that country. I could not even talk to the fellow preparing my food because he did not speak my language. I could not tell him about Jesus.

As I sat there waiting for my food, I placed my hands on the map of Mongolia and said, "God, this country is so far away, and I do not know much about it. You have to go through either Russia or China to get there, and I do not suppose I will ever get there. I do not know anyone who has been there, and I do not know anyone who wants to go. The only thing I know about the place is that the people are lost, and I want you, God, to somehow let me have the privilege of blessing Mongolia." I could not imagine how that would ever come to pass. It seemed too far away. My prayer was hardly more than a sigh, a cry from my spirit for God to visit Mongolia and do something there.

When I first got acquainted with the Mongolian restaurant, I was preparing to transition from full-time pastoring to founding the Bible translation ministry known as Evangel Bible Translators. Over the next few years, I continued to eat at the little restaurant and pray for Mongolia. My coworker, Wayne Cline, who heads Evangel Translators of France, called me on the phone and said, "Pastor, would you believe that God has brought me into relationship with a man who lived in Mongolia for many years? He was given the ability by God to learn that language, and he is translating a New Testament." He went on to say that there were no believers in Mongolia and that the man he had met had been chased out of Mongolia many years ago and was then living in Europe. Wayne said, "God put it in my heart to go visit him and encourage him, and I have been going to see him. Pastor, he has almost completed a New Testament in the Mongolian language, and soon it will be ready to go to print. What would you think about Evangel Bible Translator's taking on the project of helping him complete the New Testament and then printing it for him? I have been talking to Brother Andrew, God's Smuggler, and Brother Andrew said that I should tell you that if you guys would get it printed, he would take the copies into Mongolia."

About three months later, Wayne Cline called me again, and said, "Pastor, we have had 1,000 Mongolian New Testaments printed. They were printed in England. It is done! This was the first time in the history of the world that even one scripture had been printed in the Mongolian language. There is no church in Mongolia. There are no believers. No missionaries."

Then in the mail came my personal copy of that New Testament, the first one to ever come to America. I held it in my hands, but I could not read it. I marveled that I was holding the first New Testament in a language spoken by eight or ten million people in a country where there were no churches, no known believers, and where no known missionary had ever survived. Sometime later, I got a call from our people in Europe saying, "Pastor, we have delivered two hundred of the New Testaments." Wayne, who has known me for years, said, "Do not ask me to tell you how we got them there, because if I did, you would blab it somewhere and you might get us killed for smuggling Bibles. I have told you all I know, except there are no Christians there, but there will be, because there is power in the Book."

I knew that God was getting ready to visit that strange land so far away. Writing that New Testament cost a man his life. When God looked down and saw that old man, who for so many years had labored over a thankless task of writing a New Testament in a language that outsiders do not know, he knew he needed encouragement and he knew that someone would have to print the completed Bible. God checked his records and saw that there was not a big lineup of people asking to bless Mongolia. Apparently, there were no Bible translators, but God had a record of this preacher sitting in a restaurant laying hands on a placemat and praying, "God, I want you to bless Mongolia, and grant me, in my lifetime, the privilege of having something to do with reaching that strange land with the gospel."

Now, I recall sitting in the little restaurant and thinking, "I wish I could talk to these people, but they do not speak my language, and I do not speak theirs. I cannot communicate with them. I remember the Spirit of the Lord prompting me to pray for Mongolia. I wish that I could tell you that I went on a forty-day fast, but I cannot. I wish that I could tell you that I fasted ten days or even three days. The truth is I did not fast at all. I wish I could tell you that a mighty anointing came upon me to enter into intercessory prayer, but that was not the case. The truth of it is that while those strange people from a half world away prepared my lunch, I laid hands on a paper mat and prayed, sometimes fifteen seconds and sometimes thirty seconds. Occasionally I prayed a minute. I would say, "God, this country is so far away and so strange and so remote." I knew enough about the history of missions to know that missionaries had died there. Others had come home defeated, and there was still no church or known believers there. My heart would cry out, "Oh, God, be merciful to Mongolia. Somehow, raise up a church there." I remember making a brief prayer to God out of the depth of my spirit, "God, I cannot imagine how we would ever be involved in helping in any way to touch this nation for you and for your glory, but if in some wonderful and mysterious way you could see fit in your mercy and kindness to let us, a tiny new ministry, have a part in bringing Jesus to this country, I would like to have that privilege." My longest prayer was a minute. I would eat my lunch and go back to my office.

The years went by, and I would get reports that the old translator was doing fine. Then one day I got this wonderful phone call requesting money for the printing of three thousand copies of a trial edition of the manuscript. (A trial edition is a limited number to see if the people can read it, if it communicates, and to check for accuracy.)

Now, the New Testament is finished and printed correctly. Somehow God gave us the money, and somehow we arranged to have a little New Testament printed, bound in white with no outside markings or title. Once it was printed, we knew we would have to get the book through Russia or China, both hostile territories, into Mongolia. At this point, over two hundred New Testaments had been distributed and eight hundred more were on the way. The Word will do its work! "The people who sat in darkness saw great light" (Matthew 4:16).

Brother Andrew, God's Smuggler, heard what we were trying to do, and he said, "If you guys will do the printing, my people will take it in." That was an answer to prayer, because we had no idea how we would get the book into Mongolia. We all worked together, and the wonderful day came when the printing was finished, and Brother Andrew's people took possession of the Mongolian New Testament, and delivered it. To this day they will not tell me how it was done. They said, "If we tell you, you will stand up in one of these conventions and tell how we did it. There will be a KGB agent there and we will all get killed."

One day I got a message, "We have delivered three thousand New Testaments to Mongolia." One might say, "No Christians, no church, who is going to read them? What does God have in mind?" We did not know what God had in mind, but we were celebrating.

We got three thousand Bibles into Mongolia. One day I got a marvelous letter from a friend of mine in Hong Kong who directs a large ministry in Asia. He said, "Brother Syvelle, I know that you have had a long-standing interest in Mongolia." By then I was talking publicly about Mongolia, and he had heard it somewhere. This was before China opened, and he said, "I thought you would like to know that we sent some teams of evangelists behind the Bamboo Curtain into China, and as they were leaving Hong Kong, I ran after them and suggested that if they had a chance to get across the border into Mongolia to please do so and see if the revival in China had spilled over into Mongolia." I asked them to see if they could find any Christians there. He continued, "They have just returned from this extensive tour of China. They did get into Mongolia, and I thought you would like to know that they identified three thousand believers on the Chinese side of Mongolia." How many Bibles did we send? Three thousand. God always knows exactly what He is doing.

I was in London two years ago attending a conference of the leadership of Bible translation ministry. We have an annual meeting with Wycliffe, the Lutherans, the International and United Bible Society, the American Bible Society, the British, the Scottish, etc. The leadership of these organizations gets together annually to coordinate what we are doing so that we do not duplicate each other. We have built wonderful relationships, and that helps us to help each other all over the world. While there one of the executives said to me, "Syvelle, you were involved in getting the New Testament into Mongolia, were you not?" I said, "Yes, we had a part in that." He asked, "Did you ever meet the translator?" "I said, "No, I never met him in person. My man here in Europe handled that." He asked if I would like to meet him, and, of course, I said I would. He said, "He is about two hundred feet from you. Let us go knock on the door just around the corner and I will introduce you." Here was this man who had spent a lifetime writing a Bible for the Mongolian people. He and I had the most marvelous two hours you can imagine. I learned that he lived on the Russian side of Mongolia. The three thousand believers were on the Chinese side. He was very excited to tell me, "We had only seven believers, but this year God has given us five more so we now have twelve believers." We spent two wonderful hours together, and he was so excited that the job was finished. Both of us were amazed at how God had work over those many years to bring the Word to these people in a faraway land. As we rejoiced together, we were bonded in a passion for getting the Word to people who had never had the written Word in any form.

A few months later I got another letter from the translator, then back in Mongolia. He said, "I thought you would like to know that today we baptized over one hundred believers!" There was great satisfaction in hearing those words. I was deeply aware of his long years of sacrifice, and my great privilege of having some small part in a glorious work of the Holy Spirit. In that moment, I was aware that many others had contributed to the salvation of these Mongolians. Sometimes I wonder why God picked me, when I was an eighteen year old boy preacher, to live such *a life packed full.*

Surprise!

I had an old brother in my church who was a missionary to China for nearly fifty years. When the communists came, there was war. It was a three-way war involving the Japanese, the communists, and the Chinese Nationalist government. The Americans had to evacuate. Old daddy Bard had nine children, and they had all been raised in China. The boat they were to get on to evacuate had nine places, and there were ten of them in the family. So daddy Bard chose to stay behind. They all wept because the family feared he would be imprisoned and they would never see him again. It was like a funeral. They were all standing on the deck of the boat weeping as it pulled away from shore, and he was standing there waving to them. The boat disappeared over the horizon making its way toward the Philippines.

The boat was hardly out of sight when the pilot of the last American plane to leave China remembered daddy Bard. The plane was on the runway and there was one empty seat. As the plane taxied down the runway for takeoff, the pilot grabbed daddy Bard and pulled him into the plane. When the family got to the Philippines, daddy Bard was standing on the dock waving to them. Only God could arrange that! Now, for the rest of the story.

One Sunday morning, I asked the old missionary to lead in prayer. We had a missionary guest that morning, and I said to my guest, "Look how thin his trousers are and how shabby his clothes are; I think we ought to buy him a new suit."

I jumped up and said, "I do not want anyone here to give me more than a dollar. Give me the coins in your pocket or a dollar bill, whichever is the greater. We want to buy Brother Bard a suit."

I received several hundred dollars. One of the men in my church told me that he could buy clothes wholesale, so we put the old man in the car and took him down to the garment district. My friend made arrangements to get us into the wholesale place, and while sitting in the car with this dear old man, he said to me, "Brother Phillips, I appreciate what you are trying to do, but I do not want a new suit. I have not had one in over thirty years, and I do not want one. There is a place about ten miles from here that sells perfectly good used clothing, and if you will take me over there, I can get a fairly decent suit for fifteen or twenty dollars. If you will give me the rest of the money I will send it to my brothers in China who need help."

I said, "Brother Bard, you are going to get a suit today whether you want it or not." We bought him two suits and also shirts and ties. When he went to church the next Sunday he looked like a million dollars.

When President Nixon went to China to visit Chairman Mao, China's Head of State, they had a huge diplomatic meeting and then they had a banquet in the Great Hall of the People in Beijing that seats one thousand people. It is one of the grandest facilities of that kind in the world. It was the first time in history that an event like that was televised by satellite back to America. Now we watch CNN news and think nothing about it. But that was the first time technology was used to let us see an event live as it was happening half way around the world.

The next day daddy Bard, my old missionary friend, came rushing into my office with his eyes blazing. He pointed a bony finger at me and said, "What I am about to tell you, you cannot tell until I am in glory. If you tell now, we might get someone killed." He said, "Because of my love for China I was glued to my television set last night. While watching President Nixon and Chairman Mao, I saw one of my boys seated at that great elaborate table with Chairman Mao. He was the third or fourth one down the table. I do not know how a boy from my Bible school got in a communist government cabinet, but I know it was he. I do not know how he got there, but I know one thing, I poured the Word of God into him for three years. He will never get away from that, and he will never forget the morning that he was slain in the Spirit during the chapel service in our little Bible school, and for three hours lay on the floor speaking in tongues." Then my missionary friend said, "I will tell you what is happening. God has planted a Daniel in Chairman Mao's cabinet, and soon China is going to begin to open. You watch it, Brother Phillips. It is going to change."

It was not long until things began to change. The change is not complete, but I want to tell you that God has a lot of Daniels in that country who have not forgotten what the old missionaries did. "…and there is nothing too hard for thee" (Jeremiah 32:17).

I Am the Sinner

One day, I had to fly from Los Angeles to Birmingham. When I got on the plane in Los Angeles and took my seat, I noticed that the person in the seat next to mine was a midget—a real midget. She was a lady about three feet tall with no feet and no hands. On the nubs where her feet should have been were five little toes, and where her hands should have been were five little nub-like fingers. She was dressed very neatly, and had a beautiful smile. When the plane took off she said to me, "Mister, would you help me get my briefcase out from under the seat and into my lap?"

I said, "Sure." I picked up her briefcase and set it on her lap.

She opened it with those deformed hands got a pen and some cards, and began writing with the pen held somehow at her wrist. She said to me, "My husband and I both have master's degrees. He is a little person, too, and handicapped like I am. With all the government programs available for handicapped people like us, we could get very good jobs, making good money, but we have chosen to serve the Lord. We work with Campus Crusade. Campus Crusade is a faith ministry, and they do not pay salaries. All of us have to believe God for our support, so our friends and some churches send offerings. Every month when our checks come, Campus Crusade prints out a list showing us who gave what. I always try to write thank you notes, and I am going to take advantage of this flight to write my notes."

Finally, this little lady looked at me and asked, "Are you a Christian?"

I said, "Yes, I am a minister and the founder of a missionary organization."

She said, "I asked God to let me sit by a sinner today, because I wanted to lead someone to Jesus."

I said, "Honey, I know Jesus, but God answered your prayer. The sinner is sitting by you. You will never know how God has used you today. You will never know that you saved my ministry today. God answered your prayer. I cannot tell you what this is all about, but I can tell you that God has used you to rebuke me. I promise you that I am going to obey God."

American Hippies in Nepal

Lovie and I were in Nepal many years ago on our first visit to that country. This was during the hippie era, and there were thousands of American and European hippies there living like animals. They were dirty, filthy, and out there to get cheap drugs. Their bodies were covered with sores, and some of them were sleeping in the gutter. We saw thousands of American young people covered with sores, hungry and dirty worshipping Buddha, and spinning prayer wheels. Of all the sights we saw on that trip through India and into Nepal, I think the sight of American young people wasting their lives stirred us more than anything. We were deeply moved. Lovie and I talked to each other about what we saw. We knew that these young people were children of American mothers. These were precious girls and boys that some mothers had prayed over and loved, and we felt that we needed to do something about the situation.

We came home and I told my church what we had seen. The church was deeply moved. I told them that Lovie and I thought we needed to start a coffee house there. We could rent a storefront, serve sandwiches, something to drink, have Christian music, conduct Bible studies, and have someone to pray with these people. We felt that if they were cold and hungry they would come into the house for something to drink and eat, and we could witness to them. My church agreed that the idea was a good one. We received a big offering. Then the question of whom we should send arose. There was a couple in our church that still looked like hippies. They were not far removed from the hippie life. We all agreed unanimously that we should ask the couple to go because they understood the lifestyle.

I was young and inexperienced, and knew nothing about missions. Without any training or orientation, we just bundled up that couple, relatively new Christians, prayed over them, stuffed the money in their pockets, and sent them off to Nepal. It never occurred to us that we were doing anything other than something good. Nine months later they came back basket cases. They divorced and then disappeared. To this day, I have no idea where they are.

You see, I dropped a couple trying to do the right thing. In my zeal and ignorance, I destroyed a young couple. Believe me, I did not take it lightly. For years I would wake up in the middle of the night occasionally, and sometimes more often, and relive that story and wonder where they were, knowing full well that their blood was on my hands. In my zeal, I, a young and green pastor who did not know what he was doing, shoved that couple into a situation that they were not prepared to handle. Sometimes I would cry thinking about them.

One day a few years later, I was in India speaking to a group of missionaries, and saw a lady that I had known for years. She had gone to Nepal and opened an orphanage. Her parents were missionaries, and she had grown up in Singapore. One day, we sat in the lobby of the hotel talking. I was curious about Nepal because I had that place in my heart, and my memory of visiting there was vivid. I asked about her work and her ministry there. Talking about Nepal and her work there opened an opportunity for me to talk about my mistake. I was telling her this sad story and reliving it.

About halfway through the story, she said, "Pastor Phillips, stop! Do not say another word. I was there when that couple came. They were just as ignorant as you say they were. They were just as ill prepared. It was a terrible thing. They did not have a clue about missionary work, but you do not know the rest of the story. You just stop and let me tell you."

And this is what she told me: "In those days, it was a death sentence for anyone to witness to the Nepalese about Jesus. In their zeal or their ignorance, they either did not know or did not care; and one day, as they were crossing the street, they stopped the policeman directing traffic and shared Jesus with him. Today that man leads a fellowship of over 6,000 believers, and several dozen churches." Pam said, "So you can stop crying."

What I learned from that was that God takes our mistakes and turns them around. God allowed Pam to minister to me that day in a way she would never know. I have not awakened at night and wept over that couple again. I still pray that someday I will meet them, and be able to ask their forgiveness. The burden of that mistake and the guilt is gone, because God, in his grace and his mercy, taught me that in spite of my frailty he has a way of repairing what is broken in a fall.

Genius of the Holy Spirit

Monks, Meet the Holy Spirit

One day as I sat in my office, the phone rang. A man said to me, "I am at the Greyhound Bus Station."

Right away when a pastor gets a call from the Greyhound Bus Station all of his defense mechanisms turn on. My whole system said, "Another bum. Somebody is stranded. He will come in here and scam us out of enough money to go to his mother's funeral." You have to be a pastor to really appreciate that. All of my defenses were on. I was not the warmest soul in town, because I had been through this wringer so many times.

Soon the man said, "I just want to talk to you. I do not need anything. I do not want anything." "A new wrinkle," I mused.

He came over to my office, sat down and said, "Brother, I never met a person who was Spirit filled before other than those in my own ranks. I am a Catholic monk. I have lived in the monastery all of my adult life. But" he said, "let me go back to the beginning.

"Some kids from Evangel College in Missouri took the book, *The Cross and the Switchblade*, down to our monastery in Missouri and left it. As we began to read this book, we got interested in the Holy Spirit. My monsignor got interested in the Holy Spirit, and a group of the monks received the Holy Spirit, so the administration had a conference and decided that the way to stop this nonsense was to disperse all those who had gotten interested in the Holy Spirit, so they sent two to New England, two to the south, two to the northwest." That was just like spreading the plague.

"So," he said, "my superior was one of the two. Another brother in the order got interested, and finally the director got interested. The director had by now heard about Katherine Kuhlman, so he decided to go to Los Angeles, visit the Shrine Auditorium, and prove Katherine Kuhlman a fake. He had several degrees in psychology. He was well versed in theology, and considered himself a real brain. So, he went to psychoanalyze Katherine and the 10,000 or so people that crowded the Shrine Auditorium to hear her. With his note pad and all his paraphernalia he sat in the service and tried to make sense of all the 'nonsense' he was seeing. Finally when Katherine gave an invitation to come forward, he went thinking he would have a better chance to get a closer look. He had no idea of being healed or saved or anything. He got within about ten steps of Katherine Kuhlman; she looked at him, pointed a bony finger, and he fell flat of his dignity on the floor. When he was able to recover, he came up speaking in other tongues. They had to tell him what happened." This monk said that the director came back to the monastery and began to tell them what happened to him. The administration put him in a retreat tower, and he has been up there for months thinking over what happened to him.

My visitor said, "One day before the director was shipped off, while we were sitting on the hard benches chanting our Latin chants that the Order had been chanting for hundreds of years, the monsignor stopped us and said, 'Listen to what you are saying. You go through these chants without really knowing what you are saying. Let us stop a minute and consider what we are saying." He said that when they translated it into English they discovered that instead of a chant they were saying, "Come Holy Spirit in all of thy fullness and power." The father said to them, "Now if you mean it, if you really mean it, join me as we slowly say it as a prayer. So, for the first time instead of chanting we prayed *Come Holy Spirit in all of thy fullness and power*. When we did, it was like the upper room on the day of Pentecost. The Holy Spirit settled in upon us and about one hundred of us received the Holy Spirit simultaneously and instantly."

The Holy Spirit is a genius!

Only the Spirit of God could put it in the minds of some kids from a traditional Pentecostal school to go down to an austere order of the Catholic Church and share the book, *The Cross and the Switchblade*. Only the Holy Spirit could influence a committee to send two one way and two another until many areas were infected with the Holy Spirit. Only the Holy Spirit could put into the mind of an intellectual gentleman to get out and investigate. Only the Holy Spirit! "I will pour out my Spirit upon all flesh" (Joel 2:28).

Sounds Tricky

I gained a new insight into this recently when I was on Channel 38, the Christian station in Chicago, helping to conduct a televised missions convention. Ours was one of ten missions represented, and one night just before I went on the air, they interviewed a group called *The Slavic Gospel Mission*. Their burden is to get Bibles to Russia and to the Slavic-speaking people of Europe. One of the gentlemen proceeded to tell about how they had been successful in printing and smuggling in thousands of Bibles. "At times it gets difficult, but we have found a way to get them in." My ears perked up because I am in Bible distribution, and I wanted to hear what he had to say.

He said, "God put it in the heart of some genius in Japan to invent a magnifying glass that is paper thin, and so we learned that we can take a piece of microfilm and by using a microfilm-like technique we can print the entire New Testament on a card—half on one side and half on the other side. Then with the paper-thin magnifying glass we can read the whole thing. We have believers all over the world write letters to believers in Russia, and we enclose the letters with the New Testament cards just like we would a Christmas card. So, thousands of Bibles are mailed into Russia every day!" Now the Holy Spirit looked down over Japan and saw all these ingenious Japanese tinkering over all kind of things, and He said, "It would be nice for you to invent a magnifying glass so that my people might have the Word."

I was in another mission's convention with a missionary who told me this story: "We found it difficult to get Bibles into Russia, so we developed a plan. I am on radio in Russia, broadcasting primarily from a station at the North Pole. On my programs I read the Bible slowly and deliberately in the Russian language. Other people read it also, and we encourage the Russian listeners to copy it down. So, thousands of Russian Christians by the light of a dim lamp or a candle, copy God's Word as we read it." Just like I said, there are no closed doors, just new ways of getting in. Amen! And heaven has the ingenuity to see that it is all done and done properly.

People and Places

I had one of the most memorable privileges of a lifetime. I received a letter from France. The letter was in broken English but I could read it, and it said, "We read about you in a French language magazine published in Switzerland." At that time I had never been to Switzerland and did not know anyone in Switzerland, and to this day I do not know who published the magazine or how the information on our work was obtained. Somehow someone in Switzerland heard about what we were trying to do and took the liberty of writing an article about us. They sent us a copy of the magazine later, but I still have not figured it out. I can barely read English. What am I going to do with a magazine published in Switzerland?

The letter said, "I am one of the spiritual leaders of the gypsy church in Europe. We have 640-plus gypsy preachers. There are no Bibles in the gypsy language and never has been. We are Spirit filled. You are Spirit filled. Help us get a Bible in our language."

The ultimate outcome of that letter was that I flew to France and spoke to some 10,000 gypsies in a gypsy Pentecostal convention, an experience of a lifetime. Believe me; I never enjoyed anything so much in my life! They were great people. They were different. They never stopped talking during the church service. All eight to ten thousand of them talked nonstop right straight through the church service. Among themselves, they had a running commentary on everything that was going on, but they always said "Amen" at the right place.

The platform on which I was standing was a big trailer, and over beside it was a Volkswagen van that held all the sound equipment. During the afternoon service somebody decided they were going to work on the van, so while the preaching was going on, three gypsy brothers rolled up under that Volkswagen van, took the exhaust system off—right in church—and proceeded to wheel in a welding machine. They welded the thing back together, put it back on the van, and never moved the truck from under the tent. It was all done right in the middle of church. Nobody missed a lick. It did not bother the preacher. It did not bother the musicians. It did not bother the audience.

They Lived in Caravans

The gypsies had only about twenty buildings in all of France, so the pastors moved with their caravans, which created a problem about how to take up the offering. They might have church on Tuesday; they might have it on Sunday. To finance all this they devised a plan. I am money) in the offering. Then everybody would be given a new can, and they would start over again.

They took us on a long walk through the encampment, and we had the opportunity to visit with several of the families. There we saw hundreds of trailers, campers, wagons, and other vehicles. One group had their wagons, trucks, and trailers parked in a circle like a wagon train. There were big semi-trucks and trailers beautifully painted and waxed with chromed wheels—gorgeous pieces of equipment. Our guide said, "This family is a circus family. They have been in the circus business for generations, so when they became Christians they took the responsibility for our tent." We were under a big beautiful blue tent that was as nice as anything Oral Roberts ever had, and as big. He continued, "This is their responsibility. They put it up and take it down. They repair it when needed. All these trucks and trailers belong to the church. They are custodians of the equipment, and they move it all over Europe wherever we need it. But they are still circus people, and they are our evangelists to the circus people of the world."

They went on to explain to me that there was a tent that seated about five or six hundred people in one of those trucks, and when they would go to the circus to perform they would put up this tent over behind the circus tent and while the circus was going on they would conduct an evangelistic service for circus people. They maintained their act in the circus so other circus people would accept them.

Then they showed me a huge semi-trailer loaded with lions and bears and monkeys, and all kinds of creepy crawlers and critters. They told me that these animals were used in their circus acts. They said, "The truck belongs to the church. The trailer belongs to the church. These people are ministers, missionaries to the circus population, and all this equipment is dedicated to reaching the circus people."

I reached over and took my wife by the hand and said to her in English, "Can you imagine a deacon board in an American church having a resolution to buy a trailer load of bears, apes, and monkeys as an evangelistic tool?"

But God sat in heaven and said, "Holy Spirit, be the genius that you are. I know that you can figure out a way to reach the gypsies of Europe and the circus people in particular. Go get them!"

And the Holy Spirit said, "The way to do it is to take circus people who understand circus people, fill them with the Spirit, let them stay as part of the circus, and just keep the ministry going." I tell you, the Holy Spirit is a genius!

With Wounded Hearts

I never will forget what happened when we were in Malaysia a number of years ago. A sure this genius of the Holy Spirit directed them. Each gypsy family was given what they called "God's can," a tin can with a label on it and a slit in the top. Every day they would put the tithe from whatever they sold—baskets, pewter ware, rugs, clothing—into the can. At the big convention they would bring God's can in. The night I was there, they collected $40,000 (US little girl about nine years old followed us with a book in her hand. She was too shy to talk or approach us because we were strangers. Finally the houseparent said to my wife, "She wants to give you a book." She gave us the book, and the houseparent said, "Her father was a missionary in New Guinea. He and one of his friends were martyred. He and his wife had five children, and the mother brought this little girl here and put her in the boarding school. The mother then returned to the jungle to work with the people who killed her husband."

I did not understand the full impact of that incident until reading the book while on the plane returning home. I could not put the book down. That child had wanted to share with us her hurt, and that was her way of sharing. As I sat there on the plane, I was staggered to imagine a woman with five children farming out the ones old enough to go to boarding schools and going back 2500 miles to New Guinea and to the very people who had killed her husband. God gave her favor, and a church is there now. Believe me, that woman had to work with a wounded heart.

A minister friend of mine with whom I had preached conventions all over America is a prolific writer and has written some of the finest books Logos has published in recent years. The people who read those books never know that Jim Beal sits by the bedside of a twenty-eight-year-old son who can't move and has to be fed and changed like a baby. Jim said, "He can't talk, but he knows who I am, and it means a lot for him to have his daddy in the room with him. I pastor a large church, and I am busy. To spend time with him I put a desk and a chair in his room, and I do all of my writing and dictating in that room with my boy."

A lady came to Jim and said, "Rev. Beal, you can preach like you do because you do not know what it is to have the problems I have."

He smiled graciously but never said a word. That woman never knew the heartache of sitting by the side of an afflicted child who was dying an inch at a time. Jim Beal works with a wounded heart. Where do people get strength like that? Where do people get the courage to go on? "He giveth power to the faint, and to them that have no might he increaseth strength" (Isaiah 40:29).

What If I Had Turned Him Away?

While in India preaching at a convention, I was called on to ordain and install the leader of 600 churches. I was not a bishop, and I did not pretend to have any authority in the church, but they said, "We want you as our guest speaker to install this man." I did not know what to do having had no practice for such an august occasion. I tried to remember everything I could about any occasion like that and I threw it all together. That was the most installed fellow you ever saw. I said everything I knew to say, and prayed every prayer I knew.

During the ceremony from the back of the building, you could hear weeping. It was an older woman who finally became hysterical. No one knew why she was weeping. When the meeting was over and we were out on the grounds eating lunch, she was still sobbing. I asked my wife if she and some of the other ladies would go over to her, try to find out what was wrong, and comfort her if they could. I asked them to try to minister to her and encourage her. My wife and some of the missionaries' wives went over and began to talk to her.

Finally, she calmed down enough that they could understand what she was saying. Through her sobs she was saying, "What if I had turned him away? Oh, what if I had turned him away?" When she could speak without weeping she said, "When I was nineteen years old I came to India, alone, single, and with no financial support, just a call from God." (She was then in her seventies.) She said, "It was over fifty years ago that I walked 700 miles across India, stopping in every village and town praying, 'God, is this where you want me?' Finally, God said, 'This is the place.' I got a little house and put some furniture in it. I never intended to start an orphanage, but then the babies started coming." (In India you have to minister to children whether you want to or not.) She said, "They left them on my steps, and soon there were seventeen. I was a nineteen-year-old trying to feed and care for seventeen babies. I never once felt called to start an orphanage. Finally, one day I said, 'That's enough. I cannot take any more.'"

She continued, "One morning I got up, opened my front door and found a little bag of bones on my steps. He looked up and cried his way into my heart. I could not say no. I took him. What else could I do? I did not have a bed for him so I pulled out a bureau drawer and made a little bed for him there. I do not know how I got food for him, and I do not know how I got him through high school, college, and seminary. Now, in my seventies, just before I go to heaven, God has let me see my boy installed as a spiritual leader over 600 churches. What if I had turned him away?"

China Calling

A man and his wife came into our church, both born in China and the son and daughter of missionary parents. They had grown up in China, had gotten married, and had been missionaries in China for many years. I was surrounded by all these people who had a passion for China, talked about China, and still maintained a very fervent concern for their beloved mission field. They talked to me much about the tribal people in China, and I learned through them that there are many language groups in China that do not speak Chinese. Today, I know that there are some fifty-six language groups in China that do not speak Chinese. Only two of these ethnic language groups have any scripture in their language. Over fifty language groups, one of them with 60,000,000 people, have never read John 3:16. They have never had a gospel tract. They have never had a songbook or children's story. They have never had any of God's Holy Word or any of its byproducts in their language.

There developed a desire in my heart, not just for China, but also for those people on the backside of China who lived over the mountains and on the border of Burma, Thailand, Russia, and that vast space of Tibet, Mongolia, etc. Many times I prayed for the opportunity to be a blessing to people who lived in remote areas who have never had a dog's chance of having a crumb from the Lord's table. These elderly missionaries stoked my furnace. They really stimulated my interest. There is so much I could tell about these wonderful people. I can tell you this, I learned so much from them; they educated me.

A few years ago I flew from New Delhi, India to Hong Kong on a direct flight. It was the first American passenger plane that the Chinese government allowed to fly over their territory. Previously they had to go south and circle China. This was the first Pam Am flight allowed to come across from New Delhi to Hong Kong. I sat in that big 747 at a window while we were flying at about 35,000 to 38,000 feet, and I could see the little villages and towns below. I remembered my old friend, Daddy Bard, and the passion that God had used him to generate in me for those people. I sat there feeling helpless saying, "God, you have precious people down there. They have been persecuted and tormented, and your gospel has been hindered. I ask you to let me be a blessing to this land." I remember saying, "God, let me live long enough to put my foot on that soil."

Later, I flew into Hong Kong again from India. My missionary friend in Hong Kong met me, and as soon as I stepped off the plane he asked me if I wanted to go to mainland China. "Sure," I replied, "I have always wanted to go."

He said, "With your passport I think I can get permission for you to go in, but I have to go immediately before the office closes up on the border, and I will have to catch a train to get there. My wife will take you and your wife to the hotel." With that he grabbed my passport and took off. Later that night he came to my hotel exclaiming, "I got it! I got permission for all of us to go. We will have to get up early in the morning and take the train to the border." Then we very excitedly learned that we were going to get to take Bibles into the mainland. The next morning we filled our clothes with Bibles.

I have been serving God since I was a kid and preaching since I was a teenager, so I do not get to do many things that are illegal, and it was wonderful! We had great fun doing that. Nobody bothered us. After we got them safely over the border, we stacked the Bibles on a table in the hotel room, prayed over them, and the Chinese brothers came in to collect them and take them on into the interior. What a day!

My escort asked me if I would like to see a Bible translation project in progress. I said that I would. He said that only I could go. My wife and friends would have to stay behind. We got into an old rickety taxi, drove down one street, up an alley, down another alley, and wound around until he felt that we had lost anyone who might be following us. We stopped at a house, climbed into a loft apartment, and found three people. One was a man named Li Po John (his Christian name). He was from the Li Po tribe, and they gave him the name "John" so that they would not have to pronounce his Chinese name every time. The Li Po tribe is not Chinese. They do not speak Chinese. They are a large language group that lives on the border of Burma and Thailand, which is thousands of miles from where we were.

Li Po John told me through an interpreter that in 1906 the missionaries came to his part of China over the mountains from Burma and preached Jesus. There was a mighty outpouring of the Holy Spirit and thousands of people were saved. This outpouring of the Holy Spirit came before Azusa Street in California. He said that missionaries stayed with them for many years, and when the war came the American government said that the missionaries had to leave. He said, "By now there were several hundred churches and thousands of believers. The missionaries were getting old and as they were getting ready to leave they gathered with us for a meeting like a camp meeting. The meeting lasted several days, and the missionaries explained to us that because of the war and the coming of communism they had to leave, and that at their age they would probably never get to come back." He said, "They spread out all these papers on the altars and explained to me that one of the documents was a Li Po song book, handwritten by the missionaries and the only one that had ever been written.

They explained to us that other documents included a handwritten history of the revival among the Li Po people and their effort to write a New Testament in our language. They explained that it was not complete but that someday God would send someone to finish writing a Bible in our language. They felt that what they had done would help a translator give us a Bible. They committed the manuscripts for a New Testament to the most faithful man among them. After many years, the communists arrested that elder and tortured him until he told where the manuscripts were. They burned the manuscripts and shot the elder in cold blood, and the effort to give my people a Bible in our language went up in smoke, and it looked like all was lost."

That old man said, "From that day until today, I have prayed that God would give my people the Word of God in our language. I felt like God was saying to me, 'Go find someone.' I went up to Tibet and found Robert Morris."

The name Robert Morris might not mean anything to you, but he was a world-renowned linguist who was born in China. He lived in Burma and Thailand most of his life. He was born to American parents. His great grandfather invented the Morris Code (not Morse code). He lived in America only seven years of his life. When the war came with the Japanese, he and his brother stayed on the ground. His parents had to leave, but the brothers stayed in the jungle. American pilots flew cargo planes filled with supplies from India across to China to re-equip Chiang Kai-shek's troops. Sometimes when these planes crashed in the jungles, Robert Morris and his brother would rescue the pilots. President Reagan gave Robert Morris the highest honor that could be bestowed upon a civilian. He had retired, had finished his fifth New Testament, and was teaching part-time in a university in Tibet. The Chinese in Tibet drove him out, and at that time Li Po John found him and begged him to write a Bible for his people.

Robert Morris was the second man in that room. He told me that he had not been out of the room in three months. He walked back and forth in the room for exercise. He told me how many laps equaled a mile. He said, "I have leukemia and am very weak. I sleep for an hour and work two hours. I sleep three hours and work three hours. I work when I am awake. I sleep as long as I can, then I wake up and work some more. I work around the clock. I am not going to live very long, and I want to give these people the scripture before I die."

The third person in that room was a twenty-two-year-old Chinese lady named Lisa. She was sharp as a tack, spoke excellent English, and was highly educated. She was the daughter of a communist official. Her mother was a Buddhist. She had never heard of Jesus until an American who had come to China to teach English in a university led her to the Lord. He died shortly thereafter, and it is believed that he probably was poisoned. No one was able to prove that, but he died a mysterious and horrible death right after he led Lisa to the Lord. I do not know if there was a connection.

Lisa was in the room interpreting and translating for these two men. She also shopped for groceries, and did whatever had to be done. At the end of two hours, I was in tears. I was never so moved. For over twenty-five years, I had prayed for the privilege of giving or having some part in giving a tribal group in China the Word of God. I saw these people doing exactly what I had prayed to do. I was overwhelmed, and I cannot tell you how moved I was.

At the end of a two-hour visit, I said to Robert Morris, "How can I help you? What can I do to encourage you? I do not want to come in here and attach myself to you or this project. I just want to help if there is anything I can do."

He leaned across the table, pointed at this beautiful Chinese lady and said, "If you really want to help me, take her out of here and get her trained. She has degrees from a Chinese university, and I have taught her everything I know one-on-one, but she needs formal academic training that she can only get in America. Take her out of here."

I asked, "When?"

He said, "This afternoon."

"If I take her, who is going to help you?"

He replied, "You let me worry about that."

All of us knew that I could not take her that afternoon, but I made a commitment to bring her out of China to America. I made a commitment to get her trained to be a Bible translator. I went to work with our government and the Chinese government, and for almost three years we fought an enormous battle to get her out of China. She got her passport one day, and they took it away from her the next day. They put her under house arrest and interrogated her again and again and again. When the Tiananmen Square incident happened, they refused to let anyone out. They told her, "You will die in China. We will never let you out."

A guy from Arizona went to China to smuggle Bibles, met Lisa, fell in love with her, and moved to China. He got a job in a hotel so that he could be close to her and win her hand. When I heard that they were thinking about getting married, I had a fit because I did not know this fellow. The missionary sent me a fax telling me not to worry about the situation that the guy was a very fine man, and they all believed that God had brought them together. They got married, but the Chinese communist government said, "We are still not going to let you go." Thousands of people prayed, and suddenly the government changed its mind, and in eleven days she was out and in Los Angeles. On a Tuesday in March, I welcomed her to Dallas. On Friday, I enrolled her in college, and Saturday morning Robert Morris, who said, "When she is in America getting her education I can go home in peace," was called home to be with the Lord.

A friend of my wife invited her to a Saturday morning Messianic charismatic service in a Jewish synagogue in Dallas, if you can imagine such a thing, where about 700 or 800 people were meeting for a charismatic service. Beats anything I ever heard of! Lisa overheard my wife and her friend talking and said, "I want to go!" She wanted to do everything and go every place. I drove my wife and Lisa to the synagogue where the service was being held. I had business to take care of so I left them there and returned about 12:30 to pick them up. My wife met me in the parking lot, saying that she had gotten a phone call from Hong Kong that Robert Morris had died. She had not told Lisa because she felt that I should be the one to tell her.

I made my way back into the church, found her, got her away from the crowd, and said, "Lisa, as painful as it is for me, I must tell you that your beloved Robert Morris is with the Lord."

She screamed. I will never forget the look of total horror and sorrow on her face. The tears poured and her little body just shook with the shock and grief. My wife's friend was standing over to the side. Lisa's screams and her praying and crying had attracted attention and a whole body of people gathered around us. I explained to them that the man she had worked with and loved probably more than her own father had passed away. I asked that everyone pray for her. We started praying and the glory of God came down. I overheard my wife's friend say, "My God, it is awesome. I have heard of it all my life, but I have never seen it. I am seeing with my own eyes the passing of a mantle from one generation to another, and it is awesome!" She had no more than gotten those words out of her mouth when Lisa's tears dried, and with a radiant face she raised both hands and looked straight into the heavens and said, "My God, I accept the mantle that you are placing upon me, and I will finish that New Testament!"

It took us three years to get Lisa trained at a cost over $50,000. It is going to take a lot of money for her to go back and plug in where her beloved Robert Morris left off. He did finish Matthew, and it is being circulated among those people in mimeographed copies. This is the first time they have ever had scripture in their language. Some way God will give those precious people a New Testament in their own language. Perhaps after I am no longer able or available, someone will read this story and be moved to accept the challenge.

Editor's note:

I had the privilege of meeting Lisa, her husband, and their very lively two year old son. Lisa had finished her training, and they were preparing to return to China, or perhaps Hong Kong. I wish I could tell you the rest of the story. My brother never had a chance to tell me what happened to this couple. May his prayers be answered.

Living with the Unchangeable

Once at a PH General Conference, I heard a Colonel Reisner tell about years he spent in a Viet Cong prison. For seven years, he lived with rats and filth, not knowing what was happening in the world, not knowing whether his family members were sick or well. He was beaten and tortured. I do not believe there were many dry eyes in the auditorium that day as that man of God, told us how, that after just a few days in prison, he began to realize that God put him there for a purpose, and he decided that whatever God wanted to teach him and whatever God wanted him to do, he was going to find the eternal purpose in that imprisonment and profit from it.

He told how he and his captured buddies tapped their messages through the walls and how they prayed for each other. It was a fantastic testimony of God's keeping grace. Someone asked him if any of their Viet Cong tormentors came to know Christ. He answered that he was not aware of any at that point. I predict that within the next ten years you will see a former Viet Cong prison guard in America giving a testimony that he saw Christians under the leadership of this Colonel manifest a grace that he had never known, and that because of their testimony he came to believe in the true and Living God of those Christian men.

Several years ago we invited a kamikaze pilot to speak at the church. This man, who had been trained to be a suicide pilot during our war with Japan, stood in the pulpit and told how again and again God saved his life, how God spared him, how God protected him, and how God brought him to a place of salvation. Within the next decade, I would not be a bit surprised if one of those tormentors, one of those angry, cruel men that tormented our men, some of them to their deaths, stands right in this pulpit and tells you that he saw Jesus Christ in those men, and through their influence he felt the love of God, and is now saved and filled with the Spirit. Wouldn't that be something? I believe that it is within the realm of reason to expect God to use men like the Colonel, who knew who he was, to whom he belonged, and in whose jail he was confined.

My wife and I walked back to the hotel after having heard Colonel Reisner, and I said to her, "I have asked God to forgive me for ever complaining. I have asked God to help me never to gripe and grunt and feel sorry for myself again. I do not know anything about suffering. I do not know anything about being in prison seven long years. I do not know anything about that kind of life." And I prayed, "Oh, God, forgive me for being so self-centered and for magnifying little things in my life. God, prepare me so that if I have to face situations that I cannot change, I will not point an accusing finger at God, or lash out at life, letting it warp and twist me, but I will have the capacity to throw myself into your loving hands and let you cradle me in your tender care."

Then I had realized that at every juncture of my life, particularly when crises came, God made a principle or truth from his Word real to me. That truth being made real to me had sustained me and helped me to "get over the hump" and keep going. I discovered that what had kept me going was not some kind of an emotional experience or going to a big revival meeting and getting Brother Wonderful to lay his hands on me and falling out trembling or shaking. That had nothing to do with my survival.

What had sustained my longevity as a Christian and as a minister was that again and again when I had stood at the fork of the road and needed to make a decision, God had made scriptural principle real to me. When I had the courage to latch onto truth and obey it, I was sustained.

The Lord made it so real to me as a boy preacher that I could not produce fruit on my own but had to stay connected to Jesus and the scripture. I was reminded that he is the vine and I am a branch, and if I abide in him there will be fruit. That was a turning point for me, because I understood that I could not make anyone do anything. It was my job to abide and declare the Word of the Lord and leave the results to God and to the people who heard the Word. I did not have the right to expect even Christians to believe what I said. I just had to be faithful, stay near to God, and declare the Word of God from a pure heart. That was a major victory in my life. The Lord made real to me that law and rules and regulations and church discipline will never keep a person clean or pure. I was reminded of the time I saw a boiling spring that was feeding a pond and how the white sand boiling up was rejecting the garbage that was thrown in. There was a ring of garbage all the way around the mouth of that boiling spring—old boots, fish bait cans, beer cans, and even an old tire. The force of the water had pushed the garbage off to the side. It is when the Holy Spirit is allowed to flow through your life that the trash is pushed out. Whenever the devil comes to unload garbage, it is the force of the flow of the Holy Spirit that pushes that garbage off to the side and leaves your soul clean and pure.

An Old Missionary's Legacy

I had the privilege of speaking at the General Council of the Assemblies of God in Fiji. The great central church in the capital city had several thousand members. Down the road, there was a high school with 1,800 students. Down the road in the other direction, there was a Bible college where Fijians and other people from the South Sea Islands were being trained for the ministry. There were over 200 churches when I was there, and now there are over 400. Wonderful churches and well run as a result of tremendous missionary work. The original missionaries who went to Fiji spent forty years combating rank paganism—demon powers so strong that the guys walked on beds of coals and levitated between heaven and earth, suspended with no visible support. There are some pretty mean devils out there. This old couple went there, and for forty years they preached the gospel. One of his sons in the faith, Albert Cacau, who had only been saved a year or two, sat by the old missionary's bed holding his hand the night he died. Albert said, "The old missionary could not talk to me. He was too weak, but his spirit talked. I felt the communication flowing from his soul to mine. He was saying to me, 'Albert, son, if it is ever to be done, you will have to do it.'" Albert was the son of a cannibal. In fact, his grandfather helped eat a missionary—a Methodist missionary. We tease him that the reason he is such a great preacher is because the old Methodist preacher will not be quiet.

Here the grandson of a cannibal, one of eight converts, buries an old man who had spent forty years on that mission field. Shortly after the funeral, the Queen of England came to visit Fiji and decorated Albert Cacau with the highest Medal of Honor that the United Kingdom could bestow upon a noncitizen, because he was a war hero. He fought the communists while in the British Army. This gave him unbelievable fame, and from that the church just exploded. He said, "Standing over that grave, the eight of us, the fruit of forty years of work, joined hands in a circle. The other seven asked me to be their leader, and we committed ourselves to finishing the job the old missionary had started. Now Fijian missionaries are scattered across the South Pacific.

One of the Fijian young men that my church provided a scholarship for so he could go through Bible school saw me at a convention in Colombo, Sri Lanka. I was one of the few white faces there out of 3,000 in attendance. This big Fijian (Fijians are huge with big afros and they wear skirts and sandals) came over and sat down beside me and said, "You do not know me, but I know you. You paid my way through Bible school." He put his arm around me and said, "If you had not provided a scholarship for me I would never have been trained and I thought you ought to know that I am a missionary to the Solomon Islands, sent out by the Fijian church; and with these hands I have baptized 400 men who had never heard of Jesus. I thought I ought to tell you. You look so tired today and so alone." I was tired and at the end of my rope, but he made me remember why I keep going.

Editor's note:

> My brother was a remarkable man who kept going when some of us wondered how he could do it. At times, I wondered *why* he kept going. When his back and feet hurt so bad he could hardly walk, he boarded a plane for India or some other faraway place. "My word…shall not return unto me void, but it shall accomplish that which I please." (Isaiah 55:11).

God Doesn't Give Up

About twenty-five years ago, I went to California to pastor a church. We moved from Orange County (Orlando), Florida the day that Disney announced that he was going to build Disney World. We moved from there to Orange County, California where Disney Land is located. My son, Phil, a little guy wearing cowboy boots and a little cowboy outfit went all around the church in Orlando telling his friends that his daddy was going to California to become the pastor of Disney Land. He thought that was great. It required no consecration at all on his part. I had not been there long before I discovered that I had Mickey Mouse, Pluto, and several other characters on my board, and we went for some wild rides.

In those early days when I was endeavoring to get established as the pastor of an old time Pentecostal church, there came into my congregation a young man who was a full-blood Chorti Indian. Some missionaries had brought him there, and they wanted me to help him get trained as a Bible translator. I had said to these missionaries that if the church in Peru really believed in this fellow they should pay his airfare. Later, I was to learn that it took one hundred churches a year to raise $400 out of their poverty to buy him a one-way ticket. Then I felt like two cents that I had insisted that they undertake such a project. It was good, however, that they did that because it was their vote of confidence. He was a handsome guy with a million dollar personality, and when he arrived in my office it took me about four or five minutes to figure out that I had a real problem. He spoke very little Spanish, and I spoke very little Spanish. He spoke in the Indian tongue. We were worlds apart in communicating, and I wondered how I would talk with him. It never occurred to me that he might be limited in his Spanish. Now he is here to go to college where all the classes are taught in English, and he cannot even speak Spanish well.

This young man had been saved when he was eighteen years old. He had never heard of Jesus until he was eighteen. He had worshipped the sun and the moon like his ancestors for thousands of years before him. I knew he had potential, but I did not know how to solve the language problem. It occurred to me that he would need not only the academic training in linguistics but that he would also need theological training. I had a very good relationship with a little Spanish language Bible school that was run by the Assemblies of God north of Los Angeles. Our church had given them an organ, and I had spoken at the college. I picked up the phone, called the president of the school and arranged for my new missionary candidate from Peru to enter that college, and our church paid the bill.

It was not long until this young man was speaking excellent Spanish, making excellent grades, and making eyes at a missionary's daughter. She was enjoying it. Peru they said brought them together because she was born there, or at least grew up in Peru. He had been raised in the mountains; she had been raised in the jungles, but they did not think they had met in Peru, but because of their common background they had occasion to get together quite often. Soon they were holding hands, and not long after they wanted to get married. By now he is speaking English. When they talked to her parents about getting married, the parents were not overly enthusiastic about it because of the cultural and racial differences. The cultural difference was of more concern than the racial difference.

The parents of this young lady were very concerned. Any parent would be happy to have him as a son-in-law because he was handsome, clean, bright, and he loved God, but he was from a different world. Finally, the young lady said to her daddy, "You have been needing to go back to Peru. Go and take me with you and let us visit Romulo's parents and see what God says to us as we visit with them."

The father got enough money together and he and his daughter made the trip to Peru. They traveled by plane as far as they could go, and then it was five hours by bus, then five hours by Jeep, and the final four or five hours by horseback. They reached his village 18,500 feet up in the mountains. No trees grow at that altitude and no grass. The people live in mud and stone huts with dirt floors.

When they came into the village, the old Indian women, who wear layers and layers of clothes to keep warm, came out of their huts squawking like old hens saying to him, "Why did you bring this beautiful girl here? She will die. She cannot live here. Take her away."

That night she and her father slept in sleeping bags on a dirt floor in a hut made of stone and mud. She cried herself to sleep saying, "God, the old women are telling the truth. I cannot live here. I will die here. There is no way I can live here. Life is too harsh and difficult."

That night while they slept, the runners went across the mountains announcing, "The missionaries are here. We are going to have church tomorrow." When the father and his daughter woke up the next morning at the crack of day, she could see the torch lights as columns of Indians worked their way down the mountainside in a cold misting rain to be sure they were at the mission station for the service later in the morning.

When she finally got up about daybreak she saw her father kneeling in the mud on one side of the hut with his arm around an Indian man praying with him. She looked the other way and saw her fiancé kneeling with his arm around a couple of Indian men praying with them. She slid back down into her sleeping bag and had it out with God. She said, "God, I can live here, and I will live here. I will be his wife and coworker."

God had called him to finish a New Testament in his own language. He completed his training, and soon they were married. In due time, they went back to that Indian village taking up the project of completing a translation of the New Testament. American missionaries had abandoned the project after having worked for twenty-five years because of some of the difficult words in that language. Some of them have seventy-five letters. The white man's mind could not deal with that language, particularly the poetry of it. There is a rhythmic lilt and rhyme to the language that an outsider could not grasp. About eight or nine years later, the New Testament was finished. About two years later an Old Testament was translated.

I flew to Lima to dedicate a church that God had helped me raise the money to buy for the Indians who had no church. Over one million lived in cardboard shacks, refugees from the communists. They had come down out of the mountains and gathered around the city for safety, living in cardboard boxes and mud shacks and little hovels. On my many trips back and forth to take care of that project, God gave me a burden for those people. He gave me the chance to buy a building, and someone gave me all the money I needed to pay cash for that building. When I stood to dedicate the building, an Indian man came out of the wings with a full Bible—Old and New Testaments—in his language. I had not seen it until that time. He placed it in my hand, and I stood in the pulpit and dedicated a Bible in a language spoken by thousands of people who had never had the Word of God in their language. Thirty thousand copies of this precious book had been printed, and I was standing there holding a copy, dedicating it and the church.

Miriam's Redemption

I got on the plane to leave Peru and head back to America, and when I fastened the seat belt suddenly I said to myself, *How did I ever get involved in all this?* My mind began to run back across the years, and I remembered that when I first went to California there was a lady in our church—a widow—who had a ministry of finding wayward girls who had no home. She would bring these girls, usually teenagers, off the streets. One of the conditions for living at Evie's house was that you went to church when Evie went to church, and there would be no discussion. If you ate at Evie's table, you heard her preacher speak. That was her ministry.

I had hardly gotten acquainted with Evie, when I noticed this black-haired, brown-skinned, petite, Latin American girl sitting with her. When I would give an altar call this girl would come, stand at the altar, and pray. Then she would leave. I told my wife that she always came looking sad and left looking sad. She asked for an appointment to see me. We had difficulty conversing because of the language barrier. I could not understand her Spanish or Indian tongue, and she did not speak English well enough for me to understand her. I would try so hard to communicate, and I would pray over her. Nothing would happen and she would leave. Every two or three months she would come to see me. Then she would go away.

She grew into womanhood very fast and became a stunningly beautiful, young woman. She discovered American clothes, fast cars, and the California lifestyle very quickly. Men discovered her, and she liked the attention. Then she did not come to church any more. Every now and then Evie would ask us to pray for her. One Sunday she showed up with a man that she said was her husband. They came a few Sundays and then disappeared. She always came to the altar, and she would weep when I preached. Then I heard that she was divorced. There was another man and another one until I lost track. She seemed to be on a downhill path, and this went on for several years. She would come to church for a while and always come to the altar weeping.

This young lady disappeared for perhaps two years, then showed up again married to a handsome man from Switzerland, a scientist who had an excellent job. They came to church every service. She would come forward and he would come with her. He had not been to church since he was eight or nine years old. He had been an altar boy at a Catholic cathedral in Switzerland. He insisted on calling me Father Phillips. When she would come to the altar, he would come with her and stroke that long, black hair, looking around as if he were frightened. He seemed to be trying to protect her. Soon they had the most beautiful baby I have ever seen. By then they had a house that looked like something out of a magazine. She dressed in designer clothes. I was a proud pastor because they seemed to be making progress.

Suddenly, their world was shattered. I got a frantic telephone call that Miriam, had tried to kill herself. She was in the mental hospital. That was the beginning of a long, long vigil. My wife and I would visit her and pray with her. I remember standing by her bed as her eyes were rolled back, her hands handcuffed to the bedposts, her feet chained to the foot of the bed, and her body in a straitjacket because the doctor said that she would try to kill herself again. My wife and I would stand there and stroke her face and try to wake her up. There was no response. The doctor said that she was an incurable and hopeless alcoholic. All the time that we thought she was doing so well she was hitting the bottle.

The doctor said, "This woman has drunk so much and has taken so many drugs that she has become a drug addict." She had kept all this hidden from everyone. The doctors eventually told us that she would never be well and that there was nothing they could do for her. Her husband filed for divorce and took the baby. She lay there in the hospital day after day chained to the bed. I had to make a trip, and while I was gone somehow she came to her senses for a few minutes. We do not know how she did it but she got to a telephone and called my house. She said to my wife, "Lovie, this is Miriam. The doctors have told me that my condition is incurable, that I am an alcoholic and a drug addict. My husband has taken our baby and gone. He has filed for divorce, and the doctors told me this morning that they have filed papers with the State of California to put me in a hospital for the incurable. It is like a warehouse for the living that are waiting to die. They do not come out of there, and they are going to put me there in four days. Lovie, please pray for me."

Not only did Lovie pray for her, she preached to her. My wife is quiet and easy going, and very gentle with people, but she said to this young women, "Miriam, you have played games with God, and you have played games with me and my husband all these years. You have played games with everyone, and you will die and go to hell if you do not make it right with God. You do not have long to make that decision. I am going to pray for you, but you are going to have to do your part. You must stop playing games and get real with God."

My wife poured out her heart to God in prayer on the telephone, and ended the conversation by saying, "Miriam, do not go anywhere. I am coming to the hospital." She jumped in the car and drove for an hour and fifteen minutes through the traffic to reach the hospital. When she arrived at the hospital she found Miriam well and sane, as whole as any person around. God had totally, absolutely, beautifully, and powerfully healed her! My wife called me and said, "You have to see it to believe it! It is like a resurrection from the dead. I have never seen such a miracle in all of my life. There has been instant, total, absolute restoration."

In two or three days, I returned home, and my wife and I did not even go to the house from the airport. We went straight to the hospital. When I walked up to the desk in the hospital and introduced myself, the nurse said, "Oh, she is not in her room. She is down on the beach taking a walk." The beach was about three hundred yards from the hospital across a beautiful golf-course-like lawn. She said, "Walk down there. She will see you."

My wife and I walked across the lawn toward the beach, and this young woman who looked like a little girl, came running, not jogging, running toward us. Her feet were flying, her long, black hair was in the wind, and she looked like a nine-year-old coming across the grass. When she reached us, she threw herself into my arms, and laid her head like a little child on my shoulder, her tears staining my jacket, and she said, "Pastor, for the first time in my life I am really saved. God saved my soul, and he healed my body. I am whole and well."

Instead of going to the insane asylum for the incurable, we took her home, back to Evie's house. I called her husband, and I said to him, "We got your wife out of the hospital."

He flew into a rage, cursing me like no man has ever cursed me. He said, "Do not talk to me about that woman. She has destroyed me and cost me every dime I had in savings to keep her in the hospital. I have filed for divorce, and am on the verge of getting the final divorce decree. I have the baby, and that woman is out of my life. Do not talk to me about her." His name was Wolfgang, and with her Indian tongue she could not pronounce the name. She would call him "Wooson," so we all called him "Wooson."

I said, "Wooson, it is a miracle. It is like one being raised from the dead. Will you please come and see what God has done?"

"No!" he screamed, using a string of profanities and saying, "I do not ever want to see that woman again. She has hurt me and disgraced me."

A few days later, I called him again and heard the same tirade. A few days later I called again. This went on for about three weeks. One day I said to him, "Listen, you have been talking roughly to me, but I want you to hear what I have to say. This woman is well. God has healed her and saved her soul. She is going to be a great lady and a tremendous servant of God. She is going to make someone a wonderful wife, and if you do not have the guts to look a miracle in the eye, you are going to miss it, and for the rest of your life you are going to wonder if I told you the truth or a lie. The only way you will ever find out is to see her." I kept badgering him. I said, "Are you man enough? Do you have the courage to see her?"

"Well," he said, "since you put it like that." He let her come to his house.

She came in with tears streaming down her cheeks saying, "I hurt you, and I am so sorry. Please forgive me."

He started to use profanity again—a nonstop stream of ugly talk. He told her how no-good she was, how dirty she was, and he called her every name in the book as she stood there in tears.

She replied, "Everything you have said about me is true. I am not worthy to be your wife, but I do want to raise my baby. If you will let me, I will be your servant. I will clean the house, cook your meals, and take care of the baby. When night comes I will go somewhere else. I will not bother you. I love you, and I am sorry that I hurt you."

That set him off again. For four hours this went on, over and over and round and round. He would say the same things, and she would say the same things. Finally she gave up, but assured him again that she was not asking to be his wife, only to be his housekeeper. She got her purse and started out the door. When she did, that big Swiss-German reached out and pulled that little

Indian girl into his arms and said, "You are not going anywhere. You are my wife." Four weeks later, I baptized him.

Later, she came to my office and said, "Pastor, remember when I used to come to your office and try to tell you what was bothering me, and ask you to pray for me and you could not understand me? I was trying to tell you my story. When I was very young, my daddy, who is a leading pastor in Peru, put me on an airplane and sent me to America because he thought America was heaven. My mother was educated in America, and she talked about America. My mother died, and my daddy thought that if he could only get his daughter to America, she would be fine. When I got off the plane in Los Angeles, I did not know a soul. In my childish mind, I thought that he had abandoned me. I was on the streets in Los Angeles, making beds and cleaning floors in a motel, when Evie found me. I was trying to tell you that I hated my daddy's guts, and that I could not understand how a preacher could treat his own child as he had treated me." She was crying, and she said, "Pastor, that is what was wrong with me all those years; I did not understand. Now that I really am saved, I have to go back to Peru and find my daddy. When I find him I will be reconciled to him."

Wooson bought her a ticket, and off to Peru she went. She stayed a month. When she returned, she came into my office and said, "I found my daddy. He is a powerful man of God. When my mother died and I went away, he went to the jungles and never came out. He has two hundred churches and four hundred preachers. You have to go see him." There was no way for me to say no. I raised the money and off to Peru I went. When she knew that I had a ticket, she said that she would go ahead and make arrangements. When I arrived in Peru, she was there to meet me.

I had to hire a private plane to fly over the mountains. The little plane flew in a corkscrew pattern until it got up high enough (17,500 feet) to go over the mountain. It landed in a valley on a dirt strip by a riverbank. I was the first white man to ever be in those jungles to preach the gospel. Four hundred precious Indian pastors, some who had traveled a month by canoe down the river and up the river were there to meet me. Miriam was there to interpret for me. Romulo, the Bible translator I talked about earlier, was there to translate for me. I spent a glorious week where no white man had ever been to preach the gospel. Of the four hundred preachers, only one could read and write. I poured out my soul.

I am looking back on all of that, remembering how I got involved with those Indians, how it all started, and how I came to dedicate a Bible and a church, and I remembered just what I have told you. For the first time, it computed in my brain. Sitting in the plane remembering all of that, suddenly I knew that Miriam was not cheap or mean or wicked. God had sent her out of the jungles of Peru to find me. Standing out in front of a little mud hut-type church with no windows, her old daddy said to me in broken English, taught to him by his wife before she died, "Thank you for taking care of Miriam, and for being a good pastor to her and loving her. I did not mean to mistreat her. I thought I was being good to her to send her away. Pastor Phillips, I have four hundred preachers and only one of them can read and write. Please help me. I am seventy-six years old and will soon die. These preachers have no training, and they need you. Please come back. Please send other men of God to train my pastors."

As I sat in that plane, I knew that God had sent a twelve-year-old girl out of Peru to get me. I knew that Satan tried to kill her, and tried to kill me before the job was finished. I knew that, and for the first time in my life I understood that all of those ups and downs were satanic attacks. Then I remembered that her ancestors had a stone altar in the lost city in the jungle mountains of Peru where thousands of virgins were offered as a sacrifice to the sun god. I began to understand that demonic power and wickedness had been transmitted down through generation after generation, and that the blood of those idolaters was flowing in Miriam's veins. Hers was a legacy of demonic activity. The devil knew that if that girl ever got to me, I would join forces with that her old daddy and great things would happen.

Suddenly, I had a different attitude toward her altogether. I saw her not as a rebel, but as a messenger under siege, but God plucked the brand out of the burning. God rebuked the adversary. God stretched forth a mighty hand and brought her out of that insane asylum, saved her soul, changed her life and used her to connect our ministry with her dad's ministry. Now his people have a Bible in their language and they have churches that would never have been built in that part of the country

Miriam's mother was a missionary married to an Indian man. She died when Miriam was a little girl, but her prayers followed that child all the way, and those prayers spoke to God year after year. In that experience, I learned that sometimes Christians give up. You see, I gave up on Miriam, but my wife did not, and neither did God. "No weapon that is formed against thee shall prosper" (Isaiah54:17).

I gave this testimony in a small church in Texas, and I saw an older couple break and weep while I was sharing. After the service they came and asked me to pray for them. They said, "You had no way of knowing that Friday we took our lawyer and went to the courthouse and signed our son out of our lives. We disowned him. We cut him out of our wills and took every legal step we could to see that he would never be able to touch our property or us. We put him out of our house, and we have said to ourselves that our son is dead. He has hurt us for the last time. We took those legal steps Friday. After hearing you today, we know that God sent you to tell us that if we give up there is no one else to care. If God will let us live until Monday morning, we will go back to the courthouse and undo everything we did on Friday, and we are going to invite our boy to come home. We are not going to give up on him."

Outguessing God

An Experiment

Several years ago, I tried an experiment. One day I received a phone call from a man whom I had never seen or heard of. He said, "My name is Don Hill. I pastor a small Assemblies of God church in the mountains of Colorado. I am thirty-five years old. I am married and have three children. I am a schoolteacher. I have had an operation for a brain tumor that was successfully removed." If you are not familiar with mission boards, none of what he said makes any particular impression. First, his organization would not allow him to go to a mission field with more than two children. He must not be older than thirty-five. He must not have a major physical problem. Therefore, with the Assemblies of God Missions Board, he was disqualified.

He was calling me about joining Evangel Bible Translators to go to a mission field. We had just gotten organized, and he was reaching out to us hoping that we could help him get to the mission field. He knew that there was not a major missions board that would consider him, so he was turning to us with small hope. He continued, "I have faced reality. I am not much of a preacher. I am not going to make it as a pastor, but I want my life to count for God. I have thought about it, prayed about it, and tried to be honest in facing myself as I am. I believe that with my temperament, personality, and natural inclinations, I could translate a Bible if I had the training." After we talked for a while, he said, "If you can believe in me enough to encourage me, I think I will resign my church, quit my job, and go down to Dallas to the summer institute of linguistics and take training to become a Bible translator." Here is a guy with all kinds of strikes against him planning to become a Bible translator.

Don Hill spent three years getting a master's degree in linguistics. He and his little family looked like a band of gypsies coming down the road in an old car that was about to expire. He finally had to abandon that old car. Every member of my staff, except one, tried to discourage me from recommending him to my board for approval. His clothes were old, and his shoes were worn. He had eaten beans and rice while in school. On top of all the strikes against him, his youngest child was mentally retarded.

Could you guess where Don Hill is today? He is in the southern Philippines working with a tribe of people who have never had the Word. When I was out there to visit with them, he and his family ran to meet me in the airport. His wife, Jan, put her head on my shoulder and cried like a baby saying, "We are so blessed to be here. God has been so good to us." They are conducting seminars all over the mountains in that area, teaching those tribal people to read the Word of God in their own language.

I admire Don Hill more than I can possibly tell you, because he had the guts to face himself and the reality of his situation. He faced his limitations, and in doing so, he found strength. He said, "There must be a reason why I have this love for languages. God gave it to me, and I am going to take the strength that God built into me, regardless of the handicaps and everything that is against me, and build my ministry on that strength."

The experiment paid off for Don, his family, and those tribal people who would have otherwise never learned to read the Word. The Word is powerful, and the end result of the experiment was many changed lives.

The Black Belt

I was preaching at a missions convention in Seattle, Washington, when a mother came to me and asked if I knew her son. I replied that I did. She was like many mothers whose sons are in the ministry. My mother did that too, which embarrassed me a few times, but I am glad she was proud of me. She often asked people, "Do you know Syvelle Phillips?" She gave me a funny first name. It came from some evangelist.

The mother who came to me asked if I knew her son who was a missionary in India. I told her that I knew her son, and in fact had been with him in Calcutta not long ago. She asked if I knew his story—how he came to stay in Calcutta when no other missionaries were allowed to stay. I knew the story, but I encouraged her to tell me. She said, "When he was a little boy he liked to fight. He liked to wrestle. He was not mean, he just enjoyed the fun of it. He would twist a kid's arm, pull a kid's leg, stand a kid on his head just for the fun of it. Everywhere he went, he was into it with other boys. It seemed as though he could not help this kind of behavior. I even prayed for him because I was afraid that he was somehow possessed. I wondered how a God-fearing mother with a Christian home could have a little guy like that. When he got a little older, he wanted to take karate lessons. This straight-laced, sanctified, Pentecostal mother was horrified. He wanted to get a black belt in karate. Then he announced that he was going to be a missionary, and I knew that these two things did not jibe. How could that ever happen, a karate expert and a missionary?" His mother was very confused, and so was their pastor.

After this young man had earned the black belt, he went to Calcutta and stayed until his visa expired. The Indian authorities ordered him to leave the country within twenty-four hours. He did everything that he could to convince the authorities that he was there to bless, but nothing worked. Finally, just before his plane was to leave, the police commissioner came skidding into the church parking lot and called out to the young American, "Wait a minute, wait a minute. I heard that you hold the black belt, and I want you to teach my policemen the art of karate." The Chinese communists were causing riots and much chaos. They were marching through the streets paralyzing the city.

The Indians tend to be nonviolent, and their policemen did not carry guns. The situation had become uncontrollable, and the Indian policemen did not know how to handle it. So for the next three years, Dwight Dobson was paid by the Indian government to stay where a missionary could not be allowed to stay. He would teach karate for three hours each morning, then go to the church and do his missionary work for the remainder of the day. He had something in his hands that the church could not identify as a weapon, but God did. His sweet old sanctified mother had trouble accepting it, and I am sure that it was at times a source of confusion for him, but God had prepared him for one of the needy areas of the world. His ticket was the most unconventional thing you could ever possibly imagine. We need to get in tune with the Holy Spirit's innovative and creative work in these last days.

An Educated Janitor

When this Japanese gentleman came to my church in California, I had to get an interpreter to tell me what he was saying. He enrolled in Bible school and served as our church janitor for four years. The last week that he was with us, I discovered that he had a master's degree in nuclear physics. I discovered that my janitor was the most educated person on that campus. He had never said a word about his educational background. Through an interpreter, he told me, "I came to learn about the Holy Ghost. I came to learn the ministry of the Holy Spirit. I want to be near Pastor Phillips." For four years he polished my desk, cleaned my floors, and did whatever needed to be done, while he went to school. As we became better acquainted, he would operate the controls while I made radio programs. We did not have a fancy studio. In fact, he sat on the floor sometimes while he jerry-rigged all kinds of equipment to help me make programs that are still heard today. Finally, he helped me put a little studio in a shed behind the church. We had no idea what God had in mind.

Today, Shioshi is the manager of the Rex Humbard Ministry in Japan. When Rex was preparing to open in Japan, he wanted a Spirit-filled Japanese who had worked with an American ministry and had an understanding of radio and television. A representative of the ministry called me, and I recommended Shioshi. He runs the business with a staff of twenty or thirty. The ministry is completely self-sustaining. His wife does the translating while a Japanese actor lip-synchs Humbard's preaching.

Japanese men do not cry easily, but Shioshi came to my hotel room in Tokyo, sat on the side of my bed with tears rolling down his cheeks, and said, "Brother Phillips, if I had not worked for you, I would never have gotten this job. I learned much more than you thought I did when I scrubbed. I learned how to manage this ministry by working as your janitor for four years." He had to be willing to do what had to be done and do it quietly. Now he has a larger staff than I have. If I have ever met a Christian, he is certainly one. If there is a man in whom I have confidence, it is that man. He held credentials with a denomination. He told me that the executive board of that denomination held a twelve-hour session trying to decide if what he was doing qualified as ministry. They gave him a choice: pastor a small congregation or turn in his credentials. You have to decide what is ministry for you; no one else can decide that for you.

Trimming Toenails

There is a good Christian black man in Chicago who has a ministry of going to charity wards in hospitals and trimming patient's toenails. Can you imagine being in bed unable to do anything, with your toenails growing wild. Can you imagine a kind fellow coming along and trimming your toenails while he talked to you about Jesus? No missions board would ever come up with that one, but God put it in the heart of one of His servants to do that. He has won a number of people to the Lord while bringing comfort to many others. What if that soldier in the army of the Lord had just said, "I am waiting for Oral Roberts to invite me to speak at chapel service"? He did not sit around waiting; he got up to do what nobody else would do, and the Lord used him to bless and save.

Good Advice

There are two things I want to say, which I hope you will never forget: (1) Most of what you will do in life will be done while you are waiting to do what you plan to do. Paul is a classic example of that. He went to Athens where he was to meet Timothy. Paul arrived early, and while he was waiting, he went to Mars Hill and preached one of his most notable sermons. (2) If you do not do anything for God until you get everything in place, everything shined, and everything perfectly diagramed, you will never do anything. If you work with old veteran missionaries like I do, you will hear them say, "Well, I was planning to do thus and so, but I got stopped here in the village or town or country, and I gathered up a few orphans and began to teach. Now, there are several hundreds of them; what can I do with them?"

You do not get called to China. You get called to Chinese people, and there is a world of difference. If you are called to Chinese people, you can find them in Toronto, Cleveland, Detroit, San Francisco, London, and a dozen other places. If you feel called to a geographical area, rather than a people, you will discover that an unfriendly government can prohibit your work.

A certain gentleman with *Dr.* in front of his name told me that he was called to Turkey. I asked, "How are you going to get in? He replied, "I am trusting God." "But, friend, how are you going to get in? The Turks will likely chop off your head if you show up over there wanting to preach. "Well, I am just waiting." I asked, "Have you thought about going to Germany?" He wondered why I would say such a thing. "Because there are about one million Turks there working on assembly lines. So if you really have a burden for Turkish people, go to Germany where there are Turks and where you will not have to worry about getting your head chopped off."

When you lock yourself into preconceived notions, and you are not open to the genius of the Holy Spirit, you set yourself at great disadvantage. The least you can do to be prepared is to become knowledgeable about the sociopolitical situation in the country of interest. Free yourself from preconceived notions and tradition. Open yourself to the passion of the Lord's calling and balance that with the leadership of the Holy Spirit. Now you are in a position to discover the thrill of seeing what God will do with your life. You are looking at a man who started out as an eighteen-year-old high school dropout who was ill-prepared to enter the world of full-time ministry. Hopefully, something of my experience and legacy will be made available in print sometime in the future.

The Toy Box

Let me tell you about this couple somewhere down in Georgia. He was an airline pilot, and she was a nurse. They thought they were called to be missionaries. When they got saved, they went to North Carolina, rented a condominium, and stayed for three years seeking God's will for their lives. They applied to missions boards hoping to get appointed, but nothing happened. One morning, God spoke to Sue and said, "You are to make my Word known through the earth with Christian toys." Today, they have a company that manufactures and distributes a full line of toys designed to come against Dungeons and Dragons and Masters of the Universe, etc. When I met them, I wanted to stand up and applaud them because they had something special that God wanted them to do. They were willing to sell their house. They were willing to sell their business and to do something unorthodox. As a result, thousands of people are going to be blessed, and millions of dollars are going to be released to finance ministries, etc. If they had waited, they might still be waiting.

First Impressions

My wife was not saved the first time she saw me. Later, when I came back to her church for a revival, she had gotten saved. She was filled with the Holy Spirit in that revival. When she saw me the first time, she told her mother that she was not going back to hear me preach because I preached too loud and too fast. Her ministry has been ministering to me. She has had a powerful influence on my life. During all the years that we have been in the ministry, there has never been one problem traced to her. Me? That is a different story. I have provoked a mini-battle of Armageddon several times.

New Dimensions of Ministry

Editor's note:

> My brother lived to be eighty-three. This story indicates how his later years in life were focused on serving as a spiritual father. He did just that for over twenty years; and the influence he had cannot be measured. Many lives were touched and changed. This is a great part of his story—the story of a life packed full. I cannot imagine what it will be like when they all get to Heaven.

When I turned sixty years old, a new dimension was added to my ministry. Growing old has not been depressing for me. It has been a wonderful adventure, a grand conclusion to a life that has been blessed, and moving over into the September years of my life has not been negative in any way. Rather, it has challenged me to stay fresh and alive in the things of God. I was crying out to God, "God, I want to maximize what is left of my life. I want these remaining years to be the best, and I want to honor you more, bear more fruit, be more Christ-like, and I want to present myself in a new dedication to your highest and best for my life. Whatever you need to speak into my life, or correct in my life, or change in my life to make the next decade the most fruitful years of my life, I am open to that."

It was during that time of seeking the Lord that he spoke to me a new word that I had not heard before. It was that he wanted me to open myself up to becoming a father in the Lord to many of his servants. I had not heard that word before. Looking back, I suppose that I had begun to function as a father and as a grandfather more than I had realized.

Since I do not pastor a church, that seemed to be an unusual word for a ministry leader, but I was hearing quite clearly, "Open your self up. My servants, particularly the younger ones, need guidance. Many of them come from dysfunctional families; many of them come from broken homes, and many of them are disjointed from their church. What they need and what they are looking for is a spiritual father, and I want you to open yourself to that." That was a new unexpected word for me. I had not entertained that idea. It was a fresh thing from the Lord. I considered that somewhat strange, and I was unprepared for it. That thought had never trickled through my mind, because, in the first place, I did not figure that I was old enough. That just had not happened to me. A few days after this happened I was invited to come to a small ministers' meeting in Chicago. Thirty of us met in a hotel. It was not a preaching meeting, but a time of sharing. The format was that at the top of each hour a person would share for ten minutes whatever God was saying to him, whatever burdens he was bearing, whatever battles he was fighting, whatever sins he needed to confess. During the next fifty minutes of that hour, the group, as a whole, would respond to whatever issues the person had raised or ventilated. This was all new and fresh, so I shared that God was speaking to me about opening myself up to becoming a father in the Lord to younger servants of the Lord. I was told to say whatever God was currently saying to me, and that is what I did. There was a tremendous response by that group to this idea. It was like I had tapped a fountainhead of some kind, and there was a gushing forth of response: "There is a need for it." "The Lord is saying that to me, too." It was a wonderful hour.

During that hour, I had to go down the hall to the men's room. As I was walking down the hall, I heard footsteps behind me. I turned to see who it was, and there was one of the young preachers from our group crying and walking toward me. He said to me, "Pastor Phillips, when you spoke about what the Lord is saying to you, for the first time in my life I realized what is wrong with me. I know what is missing in my life. I was an illegitimate child. I do not know who my father was. My mother was a single parent until I was about eleven years old, and then she married a jerk. That jerk she brought home with her beat me every day, until I was fourteen and ran away from home. I lived on the streets. There someone witnessed to me and I was saved. From the streets I went to Bible school. From Bible school I went into the ministry, and I became a pastor." He continued, "For the first few weeks at a church, I get along well; but then I begin to clash with people, and I am misunderstood. Whatever I try to do seems to be wrong. I just cannot connect to people and bless them like I want to. Now I am in my third church, and I am already on a collision course. When I heard you speak, for the first time in my life I knew what was wrong. I have never had a father, and I do not know how to relate to people because of that missing part of my life." He held out his hands and with tears pouring down his cheeks he said, "Will you be my father?" I took him in my arms and held him while he sobbed.

On three occasions, right after God spoke to me; he confirmed that I ought to open myself to being a spiritual father to those who are coming after me. When I turned seventy, I had a session with God. I have done this on a regular basis at ten year intervals. I received a special assignment from the Lord when I was sixty to be a spiritual father to young preachers, and I have walked that out. Last September when I turned seventy, I asked God to give me a new mandate, a new sense of direction. It was never in my spirit to just back off into a shade somewhere, sit in a rocking chair, and let the rest of my life go by.

The Lady Who Could Have Run the Red Cross

Editor's note:

Through quickly kindled love and a short courtship, God bound two young people together for a destiny that gave them a lifetime of service that no one could have predicted at the start. God put them together with *super glue* because he knew there was a long hard road ahead. It became an adventure that changed each of them, and changed the world; and could never have happened had God not ordained it.

Syvelle Phillips and Lovie Hayes were married when she was just a teenaged girl and he in his early twenties. From the beginning, Lovie and Syvelle were partners in ministry as well as in life. She could have been successful in almost any enterprise. There were no limits to her efforts and devotion. As Lovie and Syvelle traveled to various places around the world, they confronted the needs of thousands of destitute children who were starving for food and love. Lovie founded and has directed a large childcare sponsorship ministry for over forty years. As a result of her devoted work there are children's feeding programs, orphanages, primary and elementary schools, high schools, housing for students, support for college and Bible school students, and dozens of former students who are now teachers, administrators, pastors, nurses, and other productive Christian citizens. What started as an effort to find sponsors for some hungry children, has become a ministry that has saved many lives and brought many to know the Lord and serve him.

Lovie's endless efforts to show God's love to forgotten and hopeless children has changed thousands of lives, and will in some way change the world. She has recruited hundreds of sponsors who have been blessed by their participation. Many sponsors have gotten to know their children and watch them grow up to be well-educated, productive adults who have a desire to help others. Lovie's efforts have spread blessings around the world. She has worked tirelessly for forty years so that destitute children could be fed and educated, and learn to live the life of faith, while learning to minister the love of God to others. While taking care of a family and supporting her husband's ministry, she has recruited sponsors, run the office, and traveled thousands of miles to direct the efforts of a global ministry.

Let Lovie tell some of her story:

God Loves Kids builds relationships between American Christians and formerly impoverished children in India, Africa (Uganda, Rwanda & Liberia), and Nepal. Our goal is to provide a way for Christians to act on Jesus's principle from Matthew 25:40, "Whenever you did it for any of my people, no matter how unimportant they seemed, you did it for me." We receive monthly sponsorship and support from our donors. We send the support to our trusted local partners in the countries listed above. From there, these Christian pastors, school administrators, and teachers use the funds to provide a warm and loving home and community for needy children. Our shared goal is to make these children feel welcomed into God's family, and allow them to respond to his love and grace.

The children enter our programs as victims of war, extreme poverty, AIDs, genocide, sexual abuse, and malnutrition; most grow into healthy, educated, and dedicated Christians who are ready to share Christ's love in their communities. There is no age cut off for children to exit our program. We foster a family relationship enabling our kids to grow into self-sufficient adults. We strive to build lifelong relationships and equip our kids for a life of active service for the Lord. December 2013 will mark forty years for this ministry, now operating as *God Loves Kids*. We help children in seven locations in India, one in Nepal, and seven in three African countries, plus numerous college students and pastors. We were among the first in Uganda immediately after the war; and we started with children who were left living in the forests when their parents were murdered in the "killing fields."

God Loves Kids started as a ministry of Christian Communications Commission, Inc. A 501-c-3 nonprofit founded December 1973. Its purpose is to communicate Christ's compassion to the children of the world. What started in 1973 as an attempt to help a few children has evolved into caring for thousands and is now reaching some of the neediest children in the world. In Africa, India, and Nepal we have fourteen different homes and schools. In recent years, we have transitioned into the name *God Loves Kids* because it is our passion to bring to the neglected and hurting children of the world the touch of a loving God, one who loved them so much he gave his only begotten Son to die for them. We endeavor to show the love of God to these children by providing their daily needs. *God Loves Kids* is a child sponsorship ministry that changes lives for eternity. Sponsoring a child helps change a life by giving food where there was hunger, education where there was ignorance, health where there was disease, and the love of Jesus where there was despair. To win the world, we must begin by turning our hearts toward the children.

A trip to India changed my life. Though I felt totally incapable of leading a childcare ministry, I knew I had to do something. I have learned that ability does little good without availability. I still don't claim great ability; I just have a great God who helps those who make themselves available to him. It was the first trip to India many years ago which affected me so deeply that it inspired the beginning of the child sponsorship program in 1974.

I will never forget the thousands of children who were begging for food. I will never forget seeing children digging in the garbage dump for a scrap of food. We drove by miles and miles of large sections of concrete pipe beside the roadway between Calcutta airport and the church which we visited. Almost every one of those big pipes housed a family with children. There were people everywhere, and the streets were so full of people that it was difficult to drive or walk. As our car was halted in the masses of people, we had to open the car windows because of the sweltering heat. The driver warned us not to give the children anything or we would be mobbed. One little boy pushed a ragged nub of an arm through a window close to my husband's face, and kept saying, "Love me, mister, love me." We turned away to keep him from seeing us cry. Syvelle said to me, "We are hearing the cry of the world." That little boy, along with thousands of others, likely did not live very long; we hope he learned that Jesus loved him.

Each day, the church which we were visiting took a mobile kitchen to the garbage dump to give children a piece of bread and a cup of milk. We went to the church early one morning to see 1,000 kids being given the only meal they would get that day. With tears in our eyes, Syvelle and I agreed that we must do something. That day the child sponsorship program was born in our hearts. We thought we would share what we had seen with some friends and maybe get ten or fifteen of them to sponsor a child. Soon we had fifteen; then we had one hundred. Over the years, we continued to help children through the Calcutta missions church and in ten other locations. On a recent trip, I visited the orphanage/schools that we have sponsored, where I saw the changes in the lives of children. Children that were once destitute are now pastors, teachers, nurses, village chiefs, evangelists, singers, and mechanics.

We have always believed that the way to change the world is one life at a time. One way to change a life is through small sacrifices that add up to big rewards. We saw a powerful example of this in India where we accepted responsibility for providing food, medical care, and education for some of the neediest children in the world. One little boy, a street child who was just skin and bones, was sponsored by a one of our caring Christian sponsors, and is now one of the pastors of a large church, where he is in a position to help hundreds more. Some of the children who had been in one of the schools since age three to five have now grown up. One is studying for a master's degree in history; one is studying art; one is studying political science; one is planning to be a nurse; one is studying electrical engineering; one is studying to be a machinist; one is studying electronics and telecommunications; one is a teacher, and one is going to Bible school to become a pastor. These are examples of what street children can become when touched by God's love. God's love was sponsored by caring Christians. It takes many faithful sponsors to bring our love and God's love to the children of the world.

Many of our sponsored children have grown up and joined us in the work of inviting children into the family of God. We are very proud of our children who have become adults. Many have become assets to their community, sharing the love and care they received. Some have started schools, some have started churches, and some have opened orphanages of their own. It would take a book to tell about all of the children God has allowed us to bless. Now many of those early children are our teachers, school administrators, and several of them are pastors, from our earliest efforts in Rwanda, where we started helping churches and building schools for the children who were scattered by the war. Two of our kids who grew up in the first school in Uganda have planted churches in Rwanda, and are feeding children. Richard Ssenyonga and his brother Moses were two of those kids we rescued from the forest when we first started in Uganda at the end of the war. We just got an email from Richard a few days ago saying he would be receiving his master's degree in a few days. It has taken a long time, but he has been diligent.

Our sponsors are an active part of sharing the love of Jesus with a child. We encourage our sponsors to write letters, exchange photographs, and send funds for special gifts. Some of our sponsors have experienced the joy of meeting their child, traveling to see the work of *GLK* for themselves. This is a seminal event in the lives of children who have lost their parents; finally meeting their sponsor is like a family reunion.

We respect the culture and wisdom of our school/children's home administrators to meet the needs of the children they care for in ways they find to be most effective. We foster accountability, good communication, creativity, and culturally appropriate problem solving. This atmosphere of trust is cultivated through annual visits by *GLK* staff where time is spent building a solid connection and relationship. We insist that efforts be made to ensure the children are getting the best possible care, and that funds are used wisely.

When we started, I talked to friends, and Syvelle talked about it on the radio a few times. I also shared some about it on TBN (Trinity Broadcasting Network). Syvelle was helping to get TBN's first station started, and we hosted a few programs for Paul and Jan. At that time, one of the leaders at World Vision was attending the church we pastored. I talked to him about my vision and he invited me to come to their headquarters to see what they did. I spent the day with him, and learned all I could about record keeping, and keeping the child and sponsor connected. We continued to grow and add more sponsors for many more Calcutta kids. In the early years, I simply helped people who already had a ministry to needy children as they came to me asking for help. These ministries were already feeding and educating children, and I just acquired sponsors for them. We never had to look for needs; they always found us. I will offer two examples.

In 1976, we took on sponsorship of the children at what was Miriam Children's Home in Amalapuiram, India, founded by Reverend Carl Komanpall. A group that had been sponsoring forty of his children suddenly dropped all of them at one time, and he couldn't bear the thought of sending those kids back to the streets. He asked me to help. They now have a thriving church, and they continue to be well known for their service to the poor and needy by providing food, shelter, education, and clothing.

Dr. Titus, who was leaving a good job in the States to go back to India to minister to his people, said to me, "It is impossible to establish a ministry in India without helping the children because there are so many destitute kids. Would you please help me by getting sponsors?" I have helped them for many years; now they have a Bible College, high school, church, and much more.

There is a connection between Syvelle's calling and mine. Vangpong Phom, a young man from Nagaland, was attending Christ for the Nations. He had his degree but wanted to learn more about ministry. He came to see Syvelle and asked if he would make it possible for him to learn how to translate the Bible as he didn't think his tribe had a Bible in their language. After several visits with him Syvelle said, "Vangpong, you aren't a Bible translator; you are a leader. Your dad is 104 and he will go to heaven soon and those six churches he has established will need you for a leader. You go lead the churches, and find me someone else as sharp as you and I will help him get training as a translator."

When Vangpong went home, the first buildings he built were a children's home and a school in two very remote villages, Yonguyah and Chumukedima. With the help of the Bahamian Christians, we provided the funds for this school as well as for vehicles, and support for Vangpong. The Bahamian Christians also helped provide funds to purchase a tract of land in Dimapur where Evangel Bible Translators has built a four-story Bible Translation Training Center. With help from the Bahamas, we built an elementary school and a few years later added a high school and a dorm. Now the children from the remote villages can come to Dimapur, live in the dorm, and attend high school.

Ram, from Nepal, had his higher education paid for by a lady who was a member of our church in California. That was handled by EBT of course. After his education was completed, he felt God calling him to go to Nepal to translate the Bible into one of the languages. When he got there, he was told by the government that he could not stay to translate the Bible because he was Indian. Ram contacted me immediately and told me that some of the Christians told him the government would let him stay, if he would do something humanitarian, especially for the kids (because there were so many destitute); and he asked me to please help him open a home for the destitute kids. This is our smallest home with only about thirty girls. However, Ram is still heading up the translation team while caring for the girls. About a year ago, he planted a church which is growing. He and his wife love the kids so much and take good care of them. We continue to support them.

The stories have continued for almost forty years; and the needs keep coming. My husband founded and led Evangel Bible Translators, a global missionary ministry that was demanding on both of us. Although the two ministries were separate legal entities, we worked as a team and never had a conflict. We were always supportive of each other. Since his death last October, I have greatly missed our partnership.

Editor's note:

Lovie provided interesting stories covering the life of the ministry. I had to save some of them for that book she mentioned. I have known her for all of those forty years and more, and I have never known a more devoted, energetic, and determined lady. When I chose the title for this chapter, I was totally sincere. She could have run the Red Cross. As my brother's wife, she was the only sister I ever had. You can learn more about *God Loves Kids* at the website by that name.

Miscellaneous Stories

A Bit of Personal History

In order for you to appreciate what is in my heart and spirit, I have to tell you a little about myself. It is absolutely important for me to rehearse a bit of my personal history in order for you to get a glimpse into why the fire burns in my bones and why the passion is so consistent in my life and why the passion to reach the world is such a driving force in my life.

I was born in northwest Florida, not too far from Pensacola, to a poor family. We did not know we were poor because everyone else lived as we did; we were still in the great depression. My earliest childhood memory is of living in a small house that would be called a shack. There was no indoor plumbing, no electricity, no paint, no carpet, no air conditioning, no refrigerator, two rooms, very austere. I remember my daddy coming home from work after dark whistling as he came up the dirt road that went by our house. He had walked about eight miles each way to earn fifty cents for a day's work.

After I had been in the ministry for many years, my mother died and we were going through her papers I found some bills from a furniture store where she and daddy had bought three wooden chairs for $18.00 on credit with payments of fifty cents a month. That was the furnishings for the little shack. In this pile of papers was a letter from the manager of the furniture store that said something like, "We know the times are difficult, and it is not always easy to pay fifty cents a month, but do the best you can, and we will be patient with you. After looking some more I found the bill marked "Paid in full." That was a paper trail of a long struggle for a young couple who had almost nothing. And everybody else had almost nothing.

We had no transportation so we did not have the privilege of going to church very often. When someone would come by and give us a ride we would go to church. The churches, made up mostly of women and children, were small and struggling. The buildings were crude. There was no paid pastor. There was no electricity, no water, and no conveniences, no cooling, and heating was a wood burning stove.

Every fifth Sunday those little churches would have what they called Fifth Sunday Meetings. You do not hear the term "Fifth Sunday" used much today. About four times during the year a month will contain five Sundays. When that fifth Sunday came all the churches would cancel their regular services and meet at an appointed place where these poor struggling people would worship God together and fellowship. After the morning service food would be served out under the trees. These meeting rotated from one church to another. At these meetings the preaching was usually loud and long. There was a lot of hellfire preaching, a lot of preaching to the women about how they ought to dress, and a lot of warning that God was going to get you—"You are going to hell, and God is probably glad about it." There was no music except for an old upright piano that needed tuning, and occasionally a guitar.

This particular Sunday the Meeting was held at McGowan's Chapel, a little church on the banks of the Escambia River in Covington County, Alabama. While my mother and the other ladies were spreading the food they had brought from home, I went inside the church to play. I was just a little guy, and I was exploring, looking for something to do while mother was outside. On the top of the old piano I noticed a picture—a black and white photograph—of a dignified old man wearing a black suit with a vest and a gold chain across the vest. I was attracted to this photograph to the point that I went out into the yard, found my mother, pulled at her dress skirt and persuaded her to come inside the building and tell me who the man was. I led her to the piano and the picture. She said, "That is Uncle Sherman McGraw."

I knew that I did not have an uncle named Sherman McGraw, but being a good southern boy and knowing the culture, I knew that was my mother's way of saying that he was somebody very special, and when you talked about him you called him "Uncle." That was a sign of respect. I asked, "But who is Uncle Sherman McGraw?" She said, "That is the man who brought the gospel to this community when your granddaddy and five of his children got saved." I asked why his shoes were untied. In the photograph I could see that he was wearing old high top laced shoes that were untied. I wanted to know why a man dressed up in a suit would not tie his shoes. She said, "Uncle Sherman McGraw lived a long way from our church, and he had no transportation. To preach at our little church he had to walk over forty-five miles. When he walked these long distances his feet would swell and bleed, and he often had to walk many miles barefoot. He would sit down by the side of the road and try to put his swollen feet back into his shoes before arriving at the church. Because of the swelling he could not tie his shoes."

Many years would pass before I would again remember this incident. We had a family reunion with over one hundred cousins and relatives attending. Most of us were redeemed and filled with the Holy Spirit. In the group were preachers, missionaries, doctors, educators, a scalawag and a bum or two. But by and large we were the second, third, and fourth generations after my granddaddy, a young pioneer farmer, had walked down the aisle under what is known in the South as a brush arbor, an improvised structure made of tree limbs. Sawdust usually covered the ground under the arbor.

After the reunion, I remembered the story and became intrigued with it. I got in my air-conditioned car and drove the route Uncle Sherman walked, and found that it was over 60 miles by road. Of course the roads were not there when he followed a path to the church. Later I learned that he had to swim a river to reach the church location. It began to dawn on me that someone had paid a tremendous price to set the stage for me to be redeemed. I understood anew and afresh that salvation is free, but carrying the message of salvation can exact a heavy price. Somebody pays a price to open the door of salvation to sinners. That has never changed and never will.

The young farmer who led his little brood down the aisle to be saved, following a sermon preached by the man who walked until his feet bled, was one of three boys. He was born to a pioneer farmer who had come to Florida before Florida was a state, built a log cabin for his family, and carved out a homestead on the banks of the Yellow River in North Florida. After the Civil War, anarchy reigned in the South. There was no law and order for over twenty years. Roving bands of thieves and thugs called Carpetbaggers (some were Union soldiers, some were Confederate deserters, and some were just hooligans) roamed the

South, a law unto themselves, pilfering and pillaging and commandeering whatever they wanted for their own convenience.

A band of these rogues came to my great grandfather's cabin and demanded the cow and the chickens. When my great grandfather resisted, they shot him in cold blood. He died face down with his blood seeping into the Florida sand leaving a young widow and three little boys. There was no welfare system and no government assistance. The few neighbors were equally destitute, but somehow my great grandmother eked out a living and kept her little family together until the boys were young men.

Then the Mormons came through on their way to Arizona. They were recruiting people to go with them, and one of the boys, now an adult, went with the Mormons to Arizona. Now, there is a valley east of Tucson filled with my great grandfather's offspring. Once, while traveling through that part of the country, Lovie and I stopped to visit with them.

One of the other sons became a drunkard. In my lifetime, he died in a shack sleeping on a straw bed on the floor drunk and deranged by alcohol. He died with no one attending him but a common-law wife. When he died, the preacher helped build a homemade coffin, and the preacher and his wife took his body to a public cemetery, said a few words over him, and buried him. No one attended his funeral.

The third and youngest of those three little boys became my granddaddy, the man who had come down the aisle in response to the preaching of the man who had walked forty-five miles, part of the way on bleeding feet, to preach the gospel. My mother followed her father and mother to that altar and was gloriously saved.

Today, I am redeemed and filled with the Holy Spirit, with over forty-five years of ministry behind me, and thousands of people following me toward heaven. I do not live in a valley near Tucson, Arizona. I am not a drunk. I am saved by the grace of God, and enjoying a life that has been fruitful and blessed beyond measure, a life packed full of wonderful blessings and amazing experiences directed by the hand of God..

God intercepted our family at that altar in 1906, and I am riding the crest of a wave of redemptive grace. That was no accident, and I want to tell you that I am eternally grateful to Uncle Sherman McGraw who walked forty-five miles to preach Jesus to a community of white semi-pagans with no religious heritage, except for my little grandmother who came from a very decent family.

My mother grew up loving God, and living a life of faithful commitment; and now here I am a debtor to those who came before me. The gospel reached my forefathers because someone was willing to pay the great price. When I get to Heaven, Sherman McGraw will be ahead of Paul among the ones I want to meet.

The Memory of God

I remember the story of a woman who was praising God on her deathbed for the salvation of all eight of her children. Thinking she was delirious, someone said to her, "But none of your children are Christians."

She replied "Well, the fact that I am dying does not put God out of business. My prayers will go on." She died praising God for the salvation of all of her children, and in less than a year all of them had been born into the family of God even though mother was gone.

Arnie Dirkson says that for many years he was far from God. He was involved in eastern religions and meditations and was a nightclub entertainer for over twenty-five years. He recalls that just months before he was saved, his own mother, who had been dead for years, appeared to him at the side of the bed when he was in deep, deep meditation and seeking truth. After seeing this vision of his mother, his mind began to turn back to God—the God of his mother. Hallelujah! So don't give up; keep praying

When my mother died, I wrote a letter of thanks to my uncle who had taken care of her. She had lived in a little mobile home in his backyard for fifteen years, and all those years I had felt a gnawing continuing concern because I was the width of this continent from my mother. None of her sons were there to take care of her. We could not take her grocery shopping or to the doctor. We could not see about her on a day-to-day basis, but thank God for an uncle, her brother, and his wife and their children who became family to her. I said to Uncle John, "On behalf of all the family, I want to thank you. While you took care of my mother there, I took care of other mothers here." As I cared for mothers here and ministered to them, God did not forget that I had a mother in Florida who needed care. And God arranged that. So while someone ministered to my mother in Florida, I had the privilege of ministering to other mothers in California.

Dying in Peace

Shortly after I had the privilege of leading a man to the Lord, he discovered that he had lung cancer. Two hours before he died, as I was visiting with him, he propped himself up on the bed, mustered all the strength he had and said, "Pastor, it will not be long now. I have prayed for God to heal me, but apparently it is not his pleasure to heal me. In a few days, maybe a few hours, I am going to be in his presence. Pastor, I want to live. My son is fourteen years old and I would like to live long enough to see him become a grown man—a boy needs a daddy—but I have committed myself to God. No questions asked, no reservations, I am ready to go. I am ready to go." He reached out and took my hand in his bony hand and said, "Thank you, pastor, for helping me find the Savior. I want to tell you that the peace that passes all understanding floods my soul. There is no fear." He said, "The next time you come I will not be able to talk, so while I have this strength (he had prayed for strength to talk to me) I want to tell you that I am going home to be with the Lord. I am going to be at peace with God. It is all going to be over in a little while." He continued, "When you take me up there (meaning back to his home for the funeral), the people in the community where I grew up knew me as a wicked and an ungodly boy. I ran away from home twenty years ago. Every time I went back I was drinking and carousing. When I go home again, I will be going for my funeral. When you stand in that little church you tell those people what I am telling you—that I made peace with God. Though I am dying young, and I am dying ahead of my time as men reason, I am ready to go. I am in love with God, and I am going to be in his presence." Hallelujah!

I went to the mountains of north Alabama, stood in a little Baptist church and told those dear Baptist people who had prayed for him what he had told me to tell them—that everything was right between him and God. They wept and shouted and praised God. That man could have gotten bitter. He could have said, "God, it is not fair. I just started living for you a few months ago. When I was in sin, I did not have cancer. When I caroused and cursed and drank and was unfaithful to my family, I did not have this problem; but the minute I got saved, cancer came. I have only been saved a few months, and I am going to leave my wife a widow and my son fatherless." He could have been bitter, and he could have had hatred in his heart, but the Holy Spirit had walked that babe in Christ into a fellowship with God where he could say, "Though he slay me yet will I trust him," and "When I have been tried I will come forth as gold."

Amazing Grace and Power

I was in Peru working with Indians up in the mountains where there were no missionaries. Some of these people had never seen a white man. One day the interpreter said to me, "You see that man? He is one of our finest pastors. When the gospel came to this community he was a mad man. He had been mad all his life. He was naked and his hair was long. He had never worn clothes, and had never been captured. He foamed at the mouth, and terrorized the children. He was shy like an animal. One day the old man who opened this ministry prayed the prayer of faith over him. He was instantly healed and restored, and he now serves as the pastor of a church with over 800 people." God's grace is matched with his great power to redeem, the power that comes through the cross.

The Importance of Family

The greatest tragedy in the universe would be empty mansions in heaven. An empty chair at the marriage supper of the Lamb would mock the one who died that all chairs might be filled. We are honored and privileged beyond all human beings to have gotten just a glimpse into what would really please God and that would be to have his family back together.

I caught an insight into this many years ago when my seventy-six-year-old father-in-law had a terminal illness—stomach cancer. It was like we knew that it was his time to go. There was no member of the family who knew God who had any inclination to fast and pray for his healing. That just was not in our hearts even though we loved him and did not relish the idea of his dying. It was like we instinctively and intuitively knew that this was God's appointed time for him. He lived almost to the day as long as the doctor said he would—six months. He was in the hospital in a coma and one of the relatives called and said that we should come. We had an understanding with the family that we should be called when they felt it was time. We could not stay there week in and week out because of our ministry. They called telling us that it looked like Dad was in his last days, and saying that we ought to come.

My wife and I and the boys got into the car and drove from Dallas to Pascagoula, Mississippi, a long hard drive. After driving all night, we arrived at the little hospital about daybreak. We went immediately to his room. He had been in a coma three days. My wife is the only child by the first marriage. Her mother died when she was four years old. My wife walked into the room and over to the bed and began to caress his head and hold his hand.

For the first time in three days he spoke. He said, without opening his eyes, "Lovie, you did get here." He knew her touch.

She said, "Yes, Dad, we did get here. We love you and we are praying for you."

He asked, "Where is Syvelle?"

I spoke up and said, "Dad, I am here. We are all praying for you, and we love you." I reached over and touched him.

Still without opening his eyes he asked, "Where is Johnny (an older son by a second marriage)?"

We answered, "Johnny is coming."

He asked, "Where is Wes (a younger son by the second marriage)?" He called every child's name. When we assured him that they were coming, he relaxed, and in a matter of hours he was gone.

What struck me that day was that he was not interested in real estate. He was not interested in pensions or the gossip down at the shipyard, where he had worked for so many years, or the neighborhood politics. The only thing he thought about was his family. The only thing he wanted and needed was his family. When his family was with him and he knew it, he died in peace. I thought how God longs for his sons and his daughters to come home. I thought about how far away from him some of them are and how little chance they have of ever knowing him, and I thought about how these sons and daughters, created in his image break the Father's heart. I am glad that sometime, some way, I heard his cry. I felt his heart, and I knew what he needed. I knew that I was frail and incapable, but somehow I began to understand that I was honored above most men to spend my life bringing prodigals home.

God Is Always Speaking

I never will forget how God ministered to me once. I came to Atlanta one Saturday night to preach in a church the next morning. I was dead tired. I was discouraged. A pastor picked me up in the ugliest little Pinto car I had ever seen. It was filled with garbage. He had cleaned out a little place for me to sit, so we got in and off we went to this little dumpy motel someplace. On the way he said to me, "Brother Syvelle, my wife asked me to get a jug of milk on my way home, and if you do not mind I will stop right here and get it." He whipped into a 7-Eleven and jumped out of the car to get mama a jug of milk.

When I got into his car at the airport I had an urge to turn on the radio, so when he left the car to purchase the milk I turned it on. A black brother was preaching. This fellow was really preaching. He was laying it out. I have no idea who he was. He was talking about how big God is and how good God is and how you can approach God and find everything you need. He was mightily anointed. All of this happened in about two minutes. He hit the high point when he said, "If you come to God's warehouse and he does not have what you need, he will make it for you."

I turned off the radio right then thinking, "That is all I can stand in one night." That was exactly what I needed to hear. God, in his sovereignty, had the radio set on that station, and he caused me to turn it on, and the message was delivered like dynamite in my soul. I went to bed that night saying, "If he does not have it, he will make it for you." The airwaves are always filled with voices; and God is using many of those voices to speak, but you must tune in.

The Old Church Organ

Eventually, that old church organ conked out on us. It scared me. An overhaul was recommended. One person even suggested that we junk it. Nobody would buy it from me, so I forgot it, and just this week I visited a home, and in the course of the evening, one of our families who had a $3,000 organ sitting in the corner of their living room said, "Pastor, God has put it on our hearts to give that organ to the church. It does not have a scratch on it. We owe three remaining payments of $66.00 each, and if you will agree to make those payments, we will have the organ delivered to the church."

I took their coupon book, and told about the gift in the 9:30 service. The first fellow to walk up to me after the service said, "Give me the payment book, and I will pay all three payments."

A Close Call

Two of my missionary friends, John Hurston and Ralph Byrd, went to South Korea to plant a church. They started in a ragged tent. After a while they came home to rest for a while. John asked me to go to South Korea and supply leadership for the new church. The missions' director, Brother Ketcham, asked me to go. Just as I was preparing to go, Brother Ketcham informed me that they had found a young Korean, and it would probably be better to not send an American. To make a long story short, they appointed Paul Yonggi-Cho to fill the need. Apparently, he did quite well. After all, I really did not want to change my name and learn a difficult language just to become a famous preacher. Later, when he was pastoring one of the world's largest churches, I was privileged to visit Brother Cho in California. What a blessing that great church has been to the world. I think John Hurston and Ralph Byrd will get proper recognition at the right time. I'll be recognized for a "close call."

Encounters of a Different Kind

Editor's note:

> Please be patient with me and allow me to put the following in my words. Don't hold my brother responsible for what you are about to read.

Syvelle Phillips met many people who have been involved in a variety of ministries. Some were well-known or became well-known. Some were totally unknown and working in humble circumstances. He was known by hundreds of pastors of churches of all sizes and persuasions. He was never overly impressed with anyone's status; he did notice humility for he was a humble man. Some notable encounters are mentioned here just because they help to picture the man who told all of the stories that you have read.

From *Charisma News*, I learned that Syvelle was the first person interviewed by Stephen Strang, when Steve was fourteen years of age and Syvelle was the speaker for a youth camp in Florida. Strang went on to found and lead the world's most famous magazine for the Charismatic movement and ultimately for the entire body of Christ. The magazine wrote about Syvelle's ministry several times over the years. When they wrote about my brother's death last October, they failed to mention that he was an internationally known preacher who founded and lead a global Bible translation ministry, called Evangel Bible Translators, for almost forty years. They gave him credit for a child feeding program which is part of a ministry his wife started and has lead for forty years. Lovie Phillips has a child sponsorship program called *God Loves Kids* which works with destitute children in several countries around the world. Her program was not a part of my brother's ministry, even though they were partners in ministry. Perhaps Charisma had a fourteen year old boy write about my brother's death. They had the correct information; they just did a poor job.

Syvelle appeared on Christian Broadcasting Network with Pat Robertson and Ben Kinchlow. Some of those appearances resulted in significant contacts and support for my brother's ministry. Ben personally supported Evangel Bible Translators for years. Syvelle also appeared on television programs around the country and in Canada.

In the early 1970s, Paul and Jan Crouch attended Santa Ana First Assembly of God Church where my brother was pastor. In an altar service when Paul and Jan were praying about acquiring their first television station, Syvelle gave a prophetic word that said a new Christian television ministry was being birthed. After the station was on the air, Syvelle hosted the "Praise the Lord" program a number of times. At one critical point, he made an appeal for support that resulted in significant response, with some donors bringing offerings to the station that night.

When Rex Humbard was trying to get started in Japan, Syvelle recommended a Japanese brother to the Humbard ministry to work in leadership for establishing the ministry in Japan. Eventually, the Japanese brother provided leadership for the Humbard operation in Japan. (See the above story about *An Educated Janitor*.)

From a previous story, you know that Syvelle met Dr. Cho to talk about the great church in South Korea. The church was started in a ragged tent by two of my brother's missionary friends; this was the church that narrowly escaped my brother's leadership.

Syvelle was friends with David Wilkerson when nobody had ever heard of either of the young evangelists. David became quite well-known, to put it mildly. Preaching was the passion of each. Each started from nowhere to lead lives of remarkable service and devotion. Both were greatly loved, and now they are greatly missed. One thing they shared in common was a deep concern for ministers, particularly young ministers; and each of them influenced hundreds of men and women who were called to preach the Gospel. Men like these are rare, and their legacies will live on while we wait for God to make some new ones.

I remember a humorous story about my brother and Oral Roberts. Oral was conducting a meeting somewhere down in Alabama. My brother was a young, rather brash evangelist, who feared no man. He told me that Oral, rather arrogantly called all the ministers to the front to be prayed over and blessed by the great healing evangelist. My brother got toward the end of the line. When his time came, he told Oral that he felt like he should pray for Brother Roberts first. I dare not guess how their prayers affected their future ministries.

When Jimmy Swaggert was a young man, my brother went to Louisiana to preach a revival for some of the Swaggert family. My brother never took any credit for Jimmy's fame or failure. I am certain that he rejoiced over Jimmy's recovery and current ministry.

Of course, Syvelle became close friends with Uncle Cameron Townsend, who was the founder of Wycliff Bible Translators. Their friendship lasted until Uncle Cam died. That friendship was a powerful influence on the beginning of Evangel Bible Trnslators.

Other stories could be told, but my attorney is getting nervous.

Editor's note:

A friend of my brother, and a great spiritual leader in Nagaland offered comments about his memories of Syvelle Phillips. This is one of many stories that could have been collected to support the claim that Syvelle was indeed a world renowned preacher. Vangpong and his wife worked closely with Syvelle and Lovie over a period of many years, and continue to provide leadership in Bible translation, schools, and orphanages. The following are comments by Vangpong Phom.

Pastor Syvelle was a prince of preacher who preached in various conventions and crusades in Nagaland. The people of Nagaland had a great affection for him and were fascinated with him. His messages are still fresh in the memory and the hearts of the people in Nagaland. In 2002, he was invited to preach in Nagaland Christian Revival Church Golden Jubilee program in Lungkhum, Mokokchung, where thousands of people were blessed by his messages. In March 2006, he was again invited for a big crusade in Kohima where his wonderful messages touched thousands of lives in Nagaland. He was also invited to preach in Dimapur town in Ao Christian Revival Church where hundreds of lives were touched by his preaching. Over the years, he has continued to visit and preach while overseeing the great Bible translation ministry for this region. The people of Nagaland have enjoyed his messages more than any other preacher. I believe this book about Pastor Phillips will be a great blessing to the people of Nagaland. May the Lord bless you as you write the book for your brother.

Yours in his love,
Vangpong and Narola Phom

Condensed Messages

Editor's note:

One would have to be presumptuous to attempt to condense a sermon by Syvelle Phillips. I will be even more presumptuous, and say that I think I am the only person who can do that. We shall see. I have carefully chosen sermons which add to the overall picture presented by the selected stories that make up the main portion of this book. All of the stories were told at some point in a sermon preached by my brother. Portions of stories may be repeated in these condensed sermons. These messages and many others will eventually be published in a book of sermons by one of the greatest preachers that I have ever known. I pray that God will give me the strength and wisdom to compile and edit that book.

What Jesus Said About Himself

I was struck when I read that John wrote more about Jesus than any other writer. He is the author of the gospel of John. He is the one who wrote the epistles of 1, 2, and 3 John. He is also the one who wrote the book of Revelation. I feel that Revelation is not as much a book of prophecy as it is a book of revelation—the revelation of Jesus Christ. It unveils Jesus in a new dimension. John said, "I have done all this writing for one purpose and that is that you might believe. I have been doing all this preaching for one purpose and that is that you might believe." All preachers should have that same motivation.

John wrote, "For whatsoever is born of God overcometh the world; and this is the victory that overcometh the world, even our faith. Who is he that overcometh the world, but he that believeth that Jesus is the Son of God?" (1 John 5:4). It is absolutely essential to our new birth and new life that we have faith. Faith is essential to sustaining life in Christ. A human being is not a robot that you can program like a computer to have faith. A human being is not some weird contraption that you can lift the top off his head and cram theological concepts into his brain, and then he goes the rest of his life saying, "I believe."

Sometimes we need to be able to say, "I believe because I have been able to say without batting an eye or flinching that I believe because I know Jesus Christ in a personal way. I have had a personal encounter with him, and nobody can rob me of that. Nobody can shake my understanding that I have met him in person. The reason I know in whom I believe is what Jesus had to say about himself, his own testimony concerning himself. I realize that the thing that feeds my faith is not somebody's philosophy or words of a great religious leader but what Jesus said about himself in the gospels.

There are about ten or twelve great declarations that Jesus made. I will introduce the idea and you can do your own version of it. I think one of the most profound and faith-building statements Jesus made early in his ministry was, "I am." Seven times he declared, "I am." The Jews understood that he was tying himself to Jehovah God by this declaration. Then he went on to say, "I am the way. I am the truth. I am the life. I am the resurrection. I am the door. I am the good shepherd. I am the water of life. I am the bread of life. I am the light of the world. Finally in Revelation he concludes by saying, "I am the Alpha and Omega, the first and the last." There is no other. There is none beside or between.

Every time he issued one of the statements, "I am," he followed it with a visible demonstration, a miracle, or some great teaching. He said, "I am the Bread of Life," and he proceeded to multiply the loaves and fishes to show people in a visible and demonstrative way what he meant by that. When he said, "I am the Light of the world," he opened a blind man's eyes immediately after making that declaration to demonstrate what spiritual light would mean to a person. Just as the physical eyes are opened so do the spiritual eyes open when a man receives Christ. Every one of these declarations is followed by a powerful demonstration that shows us in a practical way that Jesus was not an idle dreamer, that he was not just another speech-maker or another would-be prophet, but he was divine. When I need spiritual reinforcement I go to the New Testament and read that Jesus said, "I am." I begin to understand that through him all that God is was communicated to me, and all that I need is met in him.

You do not need to hear what Jerry Falwell, or Billy Graham, or Jimmy Swaggart, or Jim Bakker, or Paul Crouch, or anyone else thinks about Jesus. You do not need to know what I think about Jesus. There are times when you need to close out the world and take the blessed Book and read what Jesus said. That is power! You begin to understand that Jesus was not a joke, that Jesus was no pretender, that Jesus was no court jester, that Jesus was no ordinary man when he loudly and without hesitation proclaimed "I am." He covered the spectrum of every human need, and every human need is wrapped up in the declaration, "I am." Just to be sure we understand that nothing is left out, that every need is met in him, that he has addressed himself to every situation and every human dilemma, he says in the book of Revelation, "I am the Alpha and the Omega, the first and the last." That to me is faith building. I challenge you to feed on these great declarations of Jesus.

One of the great things that happened in the life of Jesus and has ministered to me so powerfully is, of course, the crucifixion. I am always deeply touched by this story. If I discover that I am getting hard-hearted and losing the tenderness of Christian love, if I discover a bit of cynicism creeping into me, if I find myself prone to be sharp and have a little acid taste to my life, and if find that I am becoming a little critical or sarcastic, I come to Calvary. There is no place to get healed like Calvary. Just go back to the gospels and read how Jesus, the Son of God, my brother, my Savior, my friend, died on a cross. Read it prayerfully and with a spirit of worship. You cannot read about a crown of thorns and a side that was ripped open and feet and hands that were nailed to a cross without that love from the written word flowing by the Spirit into your life. To me, Calvary reached a climax when Jesus cried, "It is finished!" These were the most climatic words ever spoken, and they ring throughout all ages and into eternity.

Every other religion in the world is trying to find the "bottom line" as they say in the business world. They are still trying to evolve into the final phase of truth. The founder of no other religion is able to say, "It is finished!" But on the cross Jesus cried out, "It is finished." It was not just the crucifixion that was finished. The total plan of salvation was wrapped up, sealed, and delivered. Just to linger at the cross. That is what communion is all about. It is to bring us back to the foot of the cross and to bring us back to Calvary and to make us Calvary-conscious and to hear Jesus cry, "It is finished." We know that it is all absolutely complete. God does not have to do another thing to redeem me. He does not have to have an emergency committee meeting. He does not have to have a cabinet meeting. He does not have to try to get up enough resources or get enough grace together to redeem me or the world. It is finished. All has been gathered together in him. When I read that it is finished, my faith is stimulated and strengthened.

Jesus said, "All power is given unto me." Under that general heading are so many fantastic truths. All power: The power that created the universe is given to Jesus. The power that created the heavens and earth is given to Jesus. The power over disease and sickness is given to Jesus. God invested in Jesus total power to do whatever needs to be done. All authority is given unto him. When I realize that my friend and my Savior is the custodian of divine power, that Jehovah God invested in him total authority and absolute power, that he dwells within me by the Holy Spirit, that he is not afar in some temple in India or Nepal or China or Tibet or even in Jerusalem, brother that gives me the courage to go out and face a dirty world, knowing that I can draw on the power that is in him. The power that God invested in him flows toward you in a continuing uninterrupted stream.

Hear him say, "I am the resurrection and the life," and you begin to understand that he conquered death. You begin to understand that the devil is not ultimately going to be defeated; he is defeated now. It is not a matter of heaven's gathering up enough armament and angels and going out to war hoping to prevail. We see the host in heaven worshipping around the throne, blessing the one who is worthy and saying, "Thou hast prevailed." Perhaps, the angels are thanking him for doing the job, so they will not have to attempt it. The devil will never be more defeated than he is now. He is a defeated, frustrated foe, and all he can do is writhe around like a snake that has had its head cut off. In the south where we grew up, occasionally we would kill a rattlesnake or moccasin. That snake would wiggle for hours after his head had been cut off. You can say to the devil, "Wiggle or squirm or whatever you want to do, but your head is cut off." We need to mock our adversary in a holy hilarious mockery. He was bruised, and that bruise was fatal. He is still wiggling, and we feel him squirming sometimes, but the devil will never be more defeated than he is now, because all power is given to Jesus. Live in these words. Doubt your doubts, and believe your beliefs. Reject your doubts, and embrace your faith.

If you remember nothing else I have said in this sermon, remember the crude illustration about the snake with his head cut off. He is still wiggling, but he is dead. There is no power in the world that could put his head back on and make him live again. The devil is defeated. All power is given to Jesus. That is one of the many reasons I can believe. I do not need to remember what the Psalmists said about Jesus. I don't need to think about what Isaiah said about Jesus. The Psalmists and Isaiah both said some wonderful and true things, but I am thinking about what Jesus told me about himself in his word. He said, "All power is given unto me." He said, "It is finished." He said, "I am." He said, "I am the beginning and the end." Everything he said is powerful.

Sometimes, I say that words in the New Testament get up and walk around. They walk off the page. You read and say, "My, I read that before, but I never really saw it before, and I never felt it." The words get up and start marching around and sounding trumpets. The first thing you know you have goose bumps and the tears are streaming down your cheeks. It is God's Word. He said it. These are some of the passages that have spoken to me so powerfully when I have needed encouragement and when I have needed to hear from God. When you know that he said things like "Fear not, little children, for I have overcome the world" and "Greater is he that is in you than he that is in the world"; you can go out and face anybody and anything. Another tremendous passage of scripture that has ministered to me so powerfully is Jesus's simple and powerful declaration, "I will come again." And how can we ever be unaware of his declaration, "I will build my church."

We should be tired of preachers reminding us that the world is falling apart. It is dirty out there, and it is cruel. There are a lot of mean people out there. There are a lot of shenanigans, a lot of heartbreak, and a lot of deceit. I do not need to come to church to be reminded of that. I need to hear the Holy Spirit say, "He is coming again just as he said!" I want his words ringing in my ears, "I will come again." That fact has powerfully nurtured my spirit and has had a powerful effect on me. To know that this same Jesus who went away is coming again has motivated and molded me. There is no power that can hold him back. In the fullness of time, the trump of God is going to sound. The King of kings and the Lord of lords is going to split the heavens, and we that are alive and remain are going to be caught up to meet him, and those who preceded us in death are going to be raised from the dead. I feel the power of that promise being made real to me.

Another tremendous declaration of Jesus that has ministered encouragement and strength to me is, "Lo, I am with you always, even to the end of the age." We are talking about why we can have faith. We are talking about why we can walk through a dirty and cruel world straight and strong and know in whom we believe. He said some things that are like putting great pillars under us to support us. Let me tell you now, this promise has never budged. I have been all over this world, and Jesus has kept his promise every step of the way. "Lo, I am with you always, even unto the end," I hear him say. He will never leave us nor forsake us. In trying times, you sometimes feel for God and can't find him. Sometimes you pray and you do not think he hears. But I am here to tell you that the night never gets so dark, nor the trial so severe that God leaves you alone.

Not once has he ever left me or forsaken me. Just because I am not conscious of his presence does not change anything. When I need him the most, he seems to specialize in being just around the corner. When you feel so unworthy because you have doubted or failed, suddenly there he is. You wake up in the middle of the night, and there he is. Have you ever had the experience of driving alone when suddenly you realize you are not alone, that Jesus is there with you? The Spirit of God fills the car and you are ministered to by the Spirit. Have you ever been tired, disgusted, and exhausted after working all day, and suddenly Jesus is there? The weariness goes, and a fresh new touch comes to your life. Have you ever been in church when everybody else seemed to be getting blessed and you felt like a hypocrite and a backslider? You sat there saying, "Dear Lord, what is all this? I cannot feel a thing. I am not getting blessed. I do not know what is wrong with me. I do not know what is wrong with these people. They are excited, and someone is using psychology on them. Look at them. They are singing, praying, and feeling so good, and here I sit right in the middle of this blessing not getting a thing out of it." I have felt that way, but I found a marvelous scripture in Deuteronomy 28:3, "Blessed shalt thou be in the city, and blessed shalt thou be in the field." On and on in that chapter are promises that we would be blessed. Finally as part of Moses's farewell sermon he says, "A blessing shall overtake thee." Jesus preached his own version of that when he said, "Lo, I am with you always even until the end of the age."

I have been run over by a few blessings. Unworthy, half-backslidden, discouraged, tired, disgusted, disillusioned, and not a thing in me that would generate a spiritual blessing. To be run over by a Mac truck could not be more real than when heaven slips up on you and blesses your socks off when you are not feeling really spiritual. Nothing ever spoken has the power of the words of Jesus. When things get rough, when times get hard, listen to him. He is still speaking in Africa, China, Russia, India, Tibet, Japan, the Philippines, South America, Haiti, Uganda, the USA, and to the ends of the earth, even in Alabama.

I Am a Debtor

Both to the Greek and to the Barbarian, to the cultured and the uncultured, both to the wise and the foolish, I have an obligation to discharge, a duty to perform, a debt to pay; so, for my part I am willing and eagerly ready to preach the gospel to you who are in Rome, for I am not ashamed of the gospel, that is the good news of Christ, for it is God's power working unto salvation for deliverance from eternal death to everyone who believes with a personal trust and a confident surrender, and a firm reliance, to the Jew first and also to the Greek. (Romans 1:14–16, Amplified NT)

In verse 14 in the Kings James Bible, we read, "I am a debtor." The Amplified says, "I have an obligation to discharge, a duty to perform, and a debt to pay."

The usual approach that we ministers use is to read a passage of scripture and then begin to build our case or weave a pattern of truth around that scripture. In the jargon of the clergy, we call it "taking a text and preaching from it." Often that is true. We take a text and we preach. The longer we preach the further we get from it, and we seldom get back to it. Instead of running that risk, I want to park this passage of scripture and back off as far as I can and work my way back to this verse. I will not get lost. I will be back here in about twenty minutes.

God has recently made this passage of scripture very personal and real to me. Maybe it is because I am having birthdays, but I believe that God is giving me a message not only for my life but also for the church. I believe with all my heart that I came here this weekend with a sure word from the Lord for you. This is not a sermon, not a lecture, but a message from the heart of God to the church. I say without hesitation that I expect God to honor the delivery of his word, and I expect a powerful, miraculous response. I expect God to call some of you to fulltime Christian service. I expect before we leave here today that all of you, with no exception, will reevaluate your relationship with God and your response to a lost world.

I owe my mother who taught me what I know about God and what I know about the Bible. I did not learn that in seminary. I learned at her feet when she read to me the stories from the Bible. I learned from Sister Ruby Hart and Sister Julia Still who taught me in Sunday school in my little church. (Editor's note: The three women mentioned were my teachers too, so I know what my brother speaks of when he mentions these precious saints.) Ninety percent of all I preach today was poured into me by those dear old women who never traveled far and had little formal education. Here I am, the recipient of God's grace, blessed beyond measure, confronted with Romans 1:14, knowing that someone paid a price, someone invested that I might be redeemed.

I could talk about the debt we owe our pilgrim fathers who came and carved out of the wilderness a new nation that we call "America." I could talk about the price they paid. I could talk about the people—the martyrs—who kept the gospel alive in Europe during the Dark Ages. I could talk about the disciples and the apostles and the price they paid and what I owe them. I could speak of the founding Fathers who kept the faith. Ultimately, I could talk about Jesus hanging on a cross bleeding and dying that I might be redeemed. He treads the depth of compassionate love to pay a debt that he did not owe; and, now, I must act in love to pay the debt that I owe.

A great opera singer, and Christian soloist, and I were doing some ministry together once. He and I were very open and honest with each other, and I said to him, "Archie, have you ever gone to Africa where your people came from to minister"?

He said, "Yes, I went for six weeks once, and when I got back to New York City I kissed the ground and said, 'Father God, I do not know why, and I do not understand all that was involved, but whoever it was that you put on that slave ship and sent to

America so that I could be born here and know you like I know you, I bless his memory, and I pray that you will be merciful to him. I am glad that I was born here.'"

You are not an American by accident. You are here by design, by divine design. You are not sitting in this church this morning because you deserve it or because you decided. Somewhere back there in the economy of God, a gracious God set in motion the events that put us together in his presence, and it is grace and grace alone, amazing grace.

I am faced with a dilemma. Here I am a third generation Pentecostal with a rich heritage. Somebody threw out the lifeline. Somebody kept the lights on. Somebody set the stage, and I am the benefactor. Common decency dictates that I express gratitude to God for his mercy and grace to me, and on behalf of those he used to point me to him. It would be vulgar and blasphemous for me not to give some expression of gratitude and appreciation. I am a debtor. I have an obligation. I have a debt to pay, a duty to perform, an obligation to fulfill. That was Paul's dilemma. But Paul answered his own question by saying, "I will preach the gospel to the Greeks, the Barbarians, the cultured and the uncultured, and to every strata of society." How am I going to pay the debt? Paul answered by saying, "There is power in the gospel, and I know that if I preach the gospel to the Barbarian and to the Greek and to the sophisticate, it is going to have the same effect on them that it had on me. The way I will pay the debt is not by looking back and building memorials but by looking forward and giving other people the same chance that I had. That is how I am going to honor God."

In my lifetime, I have heard of only one Memorial Full Gospel Church, and it is now dead. We instinctively and intuitively know that we do not build temples, or erect buildings and monuments in order to honor God. We may not be able to articulate the rationale behind it, but we intuitively know that building memorials is not the way to do it. The way for me to honor Uncle

Sherman McGraw, the way for me to honor Uncle Dan Dubose, the way for me to honor my pastor, the way for me to honor a godly mother, the way for me to honor the pilgrim fathers, the way for me to honor the Christ who died on the cross, is for me to believe that there is power in the gospel; the gospel that raised me from the dead and imparted life to me. I believe that if I proclaim the gospel others will believe. And their believing will become the trophy of his grace that honors him.

In an earlier service, a ten-year-old boy gave his heart to God. Whoever told me about it said, "You can just add another one of those debts paid." Soon, many of us will pass off the scene. Our spiritual offspring will be the only honor or memorial that we will want or need. You did not just hatch by the side of the road. God, in his sovereignty, intervened for you to be a child of his. When you are outside the kingdom of God, over the door to the kingdom you read, "Free. Whosoever will may come to obtain without price or money. Free! Free!" You cannot work your way in. Once you are inside the kingdom of God you will never see that sign again.

Once you taste of the goodness of the Lord, once you become the recipient of his mercy and grace, you incur an obligation. It is not just to get money. Money might be part of it, but I believe that what God wants to put in churches is the principle of spiritual truth that every one of us owes God his life and service. We should be focused and aimed at bringing others into the kingdom of God. The only honor that I can bestow upon Jesus is to bring other souls to him. We often hear the instruction to "bless Israel." The only way you can bless Israel is by bringing the message of Jesus.

We are involved in a child sponsorship ministry that my wife manages. We are involved in Bible translation. The only way I can say thank you to God is to bring some of those children off the streets of Calcutta, off the streets of Uganda, and out of the villages of Haiti to God and say, "Father, I would like to say *thank you*." I can do that knowing that there is power in the gospel. You cannot preach this gospel in vain. It will work. I am a debtor.

I have an obligation. I have a duty to perform. It is not a sad duty or an imposition. It is a joy! I embrace that debt, not as an imposition but as a privilege, because it is this gospel that saved my granddaddy from being a drunkard. Wherever this gospel is preached it will work whether it is in India or Africa or South America or the slums of Buffalo. It will work! There is power in it! God is going to find a way to let me honor his name by preaching this gospel.

A young pastor stood by the bed of a member of his church who was dying. She had thought God was going to heal her body, but he had not. She told her pastor that she was ready to die, but she was very distraught that her six children were not saved. She said, "I thought that I had prayed through," meaning that she thought she had the assurance that all her children would be saved. "But," she said, "none of them are saved, and here I am dying." The young pastor stood there puzzled, not knowing how to respond and praying that God would give him wisdom.

Quietly he leaned over her and said, "Sister, what does your dying have to do with your children being saved? When you die, your prayers are not cancelled. Your prayers, your tears, and the promises of God will still be in place. You just relax and go to sleep in Jesus. Run on off to heaven and have a good time, because every prayer you ever prayed, and every promise God ever made to you is in place. They do not lose their power when you die." Shortly, she went to her heavenly home in peace. In less than a year, all six of her children were saved. I have to believe that God let her look down from heaven to see that.

How to Serve with a Wounded Heart

The fourteenth chapter of Matthew records the story of the cruel murder of John the Baptist, and verse 12 says, "And his disciples came and took up the body (that is, John's disciples) and buried it and went and told Jesus." I have always encouraged people who have lost a loved one to go tell Jesus. Matthew 14:13–14 says, "When Jesus heard of it, he departed thence by ship into a desert place apart; and when the people had heard thereof, they followed him on foot out of the cities. And Jesus went forth and saw a great multitude, and was moved with compassion toward them, and he healed their sick."

Jesus responded to the need of this multitude, even though he had a wounded heart. I have written a note in the corner of my Bible that will always remind me that Jesus worked with a wounded heart. He had lost his cousin. John was not only Jesus's forerunner; he was a member of the family. The death of John the Baptist came as a very stinging blow to Jesus. We never think about Jesus being grieved. Remember, he wept over a friend who had died. The disciples came and told Jesus what had happened to their beloved John. We have always read that and praised God that Jesus ministered to them, that they had the freedom to speak to him, that they had the liberty in his presence to ventilate their grief and receive ministry from him. Personally, I had never thought about the dimensions of our Lord's own grief. He was brokenhearted and grieved to the point that he took a leave of absence from the crowd. He got into a boat and went over to the other side where there was a desert—a private place to be alone. He had prayers he needed to pray, and thoughts he needed to think and hurt that needed to be healed. He needed to be alone to speak with his Father.

Jesus did not have the luxury of being alone very long, because the crowds followed him. They, too, had lost a beloved spiritual leader. They, too, had been devastated by the cruel and inhumane death of John the Baptist. His head was cut off and served on a platter to appease the revenge of a lustful, adulterous woman. Can you see the indignity, the waste, the horrible hideous heathenism? The crowds that followed needed help, too. They had wounded hearts. They walked around the shores of the sea until they found Jesus in the wilderness. They sought after him, the one who could comfort. "And Jesus went forth and saw a great multitude, and was moved with compassion toward them, and he healed their sick," in spite of his own hurt. Jesus went into action when this crowd of disciples, who had followed John and believed in him, found their way around the shoreline of the Sea of Galilee to where Jesus was camped out recouping from his personal loss of John the Baptist. Jesus could have looked at this great multitude of broken-hearted people and thought, as I have many times, "I am too tired, too grieved, and too heavy-hearted. I came here to regain strength myself, and here they are again with all their needs. I can't get away. No matter where I go or what I do."

So it was with Jesus. He has gotten the message that his cousin, John has been killed. He is broken-hearted. The disciples of John are told to go back and tell the crowd that the poor have the gospel preached and the sick are healed, etc. But the crowds would not let a testimony suffice. They had to see Jesus for themselves, and somehow they knew where he was. They walked to find him. Sometimes, you must pursue him. Jesus had an option. He could send them away without ministering to them, or he could minister to them even though he had a wounded heart. This is one of the most beautiful things about Jesus. He put his own feelings aside. He put his own grief aside. He began immediately to respond to the compassion that welled up within him, and he went about his work of performing miracles and healing the sick bodies and comforting the grieved, even though he himself was grieved. Of course, we know that later he would put his feelings aside in the Garden and at the cross.

How do you serve with a wounded heart? You cannot unless you have strength coming into you from somewhere else. It is not possible for you to psychologically condition yourself to keep going. It is not possible to psyche up yourself and keep going. The believer is plugged into a source—a resource beyond himself.

How did Jesus do what he had to do? He knew the Father. He knew that Calvary was not the end. How did he face the cross without panic? He knew that the cross was just a chapter in the episode, and that the resurrection would follow three days later, and the ascension forty days later. He knew the rest of the story. How do we carry on when the pressures are heavy? Most people have had to pick up the pieces and go on at one time or another. If you have never had that experience, believe me, you will. If you wallow in your own despair, you will never make it.

If you are hurting from a divorce or a broken home, if your child has been called into the presence of God at an untimely season, if you have experienced a painful disappointment, if you have had other kinds of devastation in your life, believe me, Jesus understands. He knows what it is to go on serving with a wounded heart. He knew what it was to put his pain aside and step out to meet the needs of the mass of people that followed him. He knows where you are. He knows where you have been, because he knows what it is to suffer disappointment and hurt. Even now, we have a High Priest who is touched with the feelings of our infirmities. That's in the Book. But, he knew what his relationship was to God the Father. He knew that the future was in God's hands. He knew that we don't give in for the moment, because we are creatures of eternity. Jesus went about doing good, knowing that the cross was not far ahead of him.

One of the greatest truths that ever broke in upon my mind, one of the greatest spiritual truths that God ever deposited in my soul was when I realized that I was a creature of eternity, not time, and that what happens to me any given day is of little importance. What happens to me in a five or ten-year period of time is of little importance. On more than one occasion, people have said to me, "How do you take it? I don't see how you could possibly carry such a load. I don't see how you could suffer or undergo some of the fiery trials." I am no martyr, and I am no stranger to pain. I am no stranger to disappointment, and I am no stranger to heartache. The thing that has sustained me so many times has been a reminder by the Holy Spirit that when I was born again I became a member of the family of God, and this life is just a dressing stage on which I am getting ready for an eternal relationship with God. In the light of eternity, what does five years mean, or one year, or one more heartache? These things mean so little that they are not worth thinking about. There is hope for tomorrow. There is strength to keep going. I'm in basic training to reign eternally with the King.

I was at a college in New York for a week. Sometime during the week the president of the school said to me, "A member of our alumni is here, and before you speak tonight we would like for her to greet the student body and guests. Would you mind?" Of course I did not. He introduced this young lady who was probably in her late twenties, very petite and feminine, a beautiful young lady. As he introduced her, he said, "Cathy is one of our graduates. She and her husband went to Ethiopia as missionaries, and Cathy has just returned from Ethiopia alone. She buried her two babies and her husband in the sands of Ethiopia. We want to tell Cathy how much we love her and that we are praying for her. We know it will be hard for her, but we want her to come and say a word to you."

That little slip of a girl came to the pulpit with tears pouring down her cheeks. She said in essence, "It is true. I am devastated. I am a basket case. When we first went to Ethiopia, both my husband and I got sick, and while we were in the hospital our first born died. We were too sick to go to our child's funeral. Some kind missionaries buried our baby for us. God gave us another baby. One day when this child was two years old, we asked some missionaries friends to babysit while we made a field trip to take medical aid to the refugees. While we were gone our baby got into poison, and died, and we were not able to attend the funeral."

She continued, "Later my husband and I were hospitalized for months with some kind of African disease. Finally, we were well enough to go home. One day my husband said to me, *I am feeling better today. I think I am able to fly again.* Our helpers helped him load the helicopter with medicine and food for the refugees who were in a desperate situation. He kissed me goodbye and disappeared over the horizon. The helicopter crashed and he never came back. I left my entire family in Ethiopia."

The young lady straightened up, and you could feel the strength and fire in her veins. She said, "I will get my life back together. God will give me the grace. When this season of mourning is over, and I get the business affairs taken care of, I am going back and finishing what we started. It was not just my husband's call. It was our call, and my part of it is not finished." She will serve with a wounded heart; and He will understand.

We Need to Testify

We find some powerful words in Revelation 12:10–11: "Then I heard a voice saying in heaven, Now is salvation and strength and the kingdom of our God and the power of his Christ come. For the accuser of our brethren who accused them before our God day and night has been cast down. And they overcame him by the blood of the Lamb, and by the word of their testimony, and they did not love their lives to the death."

There are three major components to being an overcomer: (1) The blood of the Lamb, (2) The word of our testimony, and (3) Not loving our lives but laying them on the line. Those three comprise a wonderful formula for absolute victory. As long as you love your life and hang onto it, something is missing. As long as you do not verbalize what God is doing, something is missing. It strikes me as being quite profound that the word of our testimony is linked and associated with the power that is in the blood of the Lamb. The shed blood of Jesus Christ is powerful unto our redemption, and this verse puts beside that the power of our testimony.

God has really been dealing with my heart about how we ought to talk to each other about what he is doing. *We need to testify.* To testify means to verbalize and articulate what God has done and what God is doing in our lives. When Lazarus died, by the natural way of computing, Jesus was late getting there. He got there just in time for a resurrection, but as men count it, he was late. When he came to the family home, Lazarus's sister came out to meet Jesus, and she said, "Lord, if you had been here." Then Jesus tried to move her out of the past and into the present. He began to talk to her about resurrection, and she said, "Lord, I know that in the last day there will be a resurrection, and my brother will live again." She made the classic mistake that God's people make many times and that is to put him in the past. The next thing she did was to put him into the far distant future. That left the *now* untouched. Jesus was faced with a challenge of moving her out of the past and into the present, out of the future and into the present. That looks like a challenge for the Holy Spirit.

There are large segments of the Christian church that live in the past. It is history, something that happened hundreds or thousands of years ago. The days of miracles are over. The day of the apostles and prophets is over. Everything of divine origin happened way back. If you ever move those people, they are likely to make the same mistake that Martha made and that is to skid right past today and say, "Out there in the Millennium, in the rapture, way out there somewhere Jesus is going to come back to rule and reign as King of Kings and Lord of Lords." That leaves the present untouched. It is not the sweet by and by that is giving me trouble. It is the dirty now and now. While I need to be aware of divine history, I need a God that is alive today. I need a God that is active today. I need a God that is relevant today, relevant to me where I am and to what I need, and to the battles I fight. I do not want to be ignorant of history, and I do not want to be ignorant of the future, but I don't want to make the mistake of parking Jesus at either extreme. He is there. He was there. He will be there, but he wants to be here *now*.

One of the ways we can help each other and edify each other and make each other aware that God is a God of the present, a God of today, is to *talk* about what he is doing. It seems a shame that Christian men find it easier to talk about sports than to talk about what God is doing in their lives. Let me tell one little story to illustrate the power of testimony. When my two boys were teenagers, we were having lunch in a restaurant, and talking about how good God had been to us. I glanced up to see a burly black man coming toward us. As he approached, he said, "Excuse me fellows, but I heard you talking about God being good. I once knew the Lord, but I left him." He knelt down by my chair and began to confess and repent. We joined him in prayer, and rejoiced with him as he came back to the Lord. My boys and I were amazed that our testifying to each other had been used by the Holy Spirit to move that big bus driver back to God.

It is a shame that it is easier for ladies to talk about recipes and the latest news around town than it is to talk about what God has done and is doing. One of the things God has spoken to me about concerning my personal ministry is that I need to talk to his people about what he is doing now. I need to tell them that there is power in testimony. I need to tell them that there is power in rehearsing the acts of God. I need to tell them that there is power in erecting a marker and saying, "This is my Ebenezer. Hitherto God has helped us." There is power in that.

I have been labeled a storyteller. People talk about the missionary stories I tell. However, I am a preacher, and I love to take the Bible and a text and dig out the meat and share it with God's people. Some years ago I was preaching at a ministers' conference in Georgia. During the break I went into the restroom, and while I was in there two preachers came in. They, of course, did not know that I was in there, and to this day they do not know. One said to the other, "This Syvelle Phillips used to be a great preacher, but as he has gotten older he has stopped preaching and became a storyteller. He is a great storyteller, but it is a shame that a great preacher would turn into a storyteller." You know how it is to hear something that sends a flash of heat over you. His comments stung and startled me. For a minute or two I thought about what they had said, and it made me angry. Then suddenly I started laughing. The Holy Spirit ministered to my heart. He said, "Who was invited to preach at this convention, the old storyteller or those two turkeys that came in here?" That really comforted my heart.

Editor's note:

> My brother just kept on telling those stories. Now, in this book those stories will continue to be a blessing to many for years to come. Perhaps those "two turkeys" will read this. This book was published so my brother's stories could stay alive and bless. He will be testifying for a long time to many who read his stories.

I was wrestling with the question of whether or not I should continue to give testimonies, when the Lord spoke to my heart that he wants those of us who have paid the price and made the journey and are victorious survivors, to stand up and tell the good story of his faithfulness and his grace, and say to young Christians, "Come on, you can make it. There is a God on the throne." I have a lot of miles on my odometer and a lot of years behind me, and I am not just a survivor but a victorious survivor. God has again and again said to me in the last few years, "Tell my people what I am doing. Let them rejoice in it. Let them celebrate that I am not only a God of the distant past, not only a God of the future out there somewhere, but I am a God who is alive and well and on the move in the earth today.

That is why we take the time to share. We want to report that there is a God who still hears a Hindu girl's cry. There is a God who still reveals himself where no missionary has ever been or will ever go. That is a good report! It is a great report for my wife, Lovie, to tell you about nine and ten-year-old boys whose parents had been slaughtered and who were found living under trees eating roots and bark, but who are now preaching the gospel and establishing churches. That is a good report! That is something to celebrate! That is something to rejoice over! There is a God in heaven who is on the move in this world.

It is true that the books of the world could not contain what he did in the past, and the future is too glorious for us to even imagine, but I am not out there in the Millennium, but I am not way back there with Abraham, Moses, and Jacob. I am here! I am here where demons are on the prowl. I am here where our Christian values are under attack. I am here where there is confusion and doubt and unbelief and where there is sickness and satanic oppression, and I need to know that there is a God who cares about what is going on *now*. I can tell you that there is a God who is well and on the throne and acting today with great and wonderful power. The precious Holy Spirit is here with us and in us to perform the mighty acts of God.

What Would You Do with Lazarus?

"There was a certain rich man, which was clothed in purple and fine linen, and fared sumptuously every day; And there was a certain beggar named Lazarus, which was laid at his gate full of sores, and desiring to be fed with the crumbs which fell from the rich man's table; moreover the dogs came and licked his sores" (Luke 16:19–21).

I want to ask you a question. If God put a Lazarus on your doorstep, what would you do with him? I do not enjoy having a

Lazarus put in my life, but when I look back and see that he made me pray when I would not have prayed otherwise, and he forced me to give when I would not have given otherwise, and he forced me to think about things that I would not have thought about otherwise, and forced me to come to grips with issues that made a difference for me when those issues were settled in my own mind and value system, I realize how much I needed a Lazarus.

I was in Spokane, Washington speaking at a Christmas camp meeting, and in the course of my sharing; I said something about my long-standing burden for Cuba and my desire to somehow find a way to be a blessing to Cuba. I shared that I had never been able to fulfill that vision or dream. After the service the host pastor said to me, "You mentioned when you were talking about Cuba that there is a young man working with you who takes groups of young people to Cuba." I had dreamed about doing that for years, and now it was happening. This young man was taking groups of teenagers through Mexico into Cuba for ministry. This pastor said, "We have had that desire, and we would like to send a group of our young people to Cuba for ministry. Next year when you come back bring that young missionary with you. We would like to meet him, and maybe we can work out an arrangement where he could lead a group of our young people on a short-term mission trip to Cuba." All was fine and good.

The next year when I went back to speak at that conference I did take the young missionary. In fact, he arrived about three days before I did. To my surprise, when I arrived I discovered that the girls in the church were all falling in love with him. They were hovering over him and taking care of him like mother hens. When I started to preach, I looked up to see them bringing him in on a cot. He told them that he did not get to hear me preach often, and though he was weak he would like to hear Pastor Phillips preach if they could get him to the church. Here were a dozen young people hovering over this guy fanning him, giving him drinks, and taking care of him, which he was thoroughly enjoying. His condition seemed to deteriorate, so after a while I asked a young doctor in the church to examine the guy and find out what was wrong with him. This was the second time I had been through this with him. I said, "Don't leave any stone unturned. Do blood tests, x-rays, etc. Find out what is wrong with him."

Two or three days went by before I heard from the doctor. Then he called me, and this is what he said, "Pastor, I am sorry to have to tell you this, but your missionary has AIDS." You cannot imagine how shocked and embarrassed I was. The doctor went on to say that the guy had gotten the disease the old fashioned way. I was devastated—for him, for me, and the mission I represented, because that church considered me a man of integrity, a man that they could depend on, and I had brought in a hypocrite and presented him to them as one of our missionaries. I do not know how he got through our screening process, because we do not accept just anybody. We must have medical reports on candidates. But, somehow he got through the system, and he carried our name.

I was devastated for the young people who had come to look up to him. He was a very charming person. I was also devastated for all the young people he had been taking to Cuba. I was broken hearted, and you cannot imagine the complex problems I saw myself facing. Will the parents or pastors of some of these young people who had gone on trips with him bring suit against our ministry? I was in a predicament. I rushed to the pastor saying, "Oh, pastor, I did not know. Please forgive me."

He stopped me and said, "Brother Syvelle, stop. We know you would not have done this deliberately. We know that you are broken-hearted about this. Stop feeling guilty. We do not hold you responsible." He continued, "And furthermore what you do not know is that a year ago I said to my staff and the church, *AIDS is coming*. We have been praying for one year that God would teach us how to minister to people with AIDS, so this man came to us in answer to our prayers, not because of your carelessness. We have had no experience with working with homosexuals and AIDS victims, and we have been praying that God would teach us, because we want to receive these people in God's name and minister to them God's way. So, to be frank with you, we never expected that person to be a missionary, but that is who God has sent us, and we have received him in the name of Jesus. Now we are going to let God teach us how to love a man that is difficult to love."

The young missionary was admitted to the hospital, and the church arranged to take care of a $40,000 hospital bill. They rented an apartment and put him in it and kept him until he died. He was not easy to deal with. In his dying days he was ill-tempered, contrary, and mean-spirited. They prayed over him, loved him, fed him, took care of him, and they learned. They said, "God sent us our Lazarus, and we have fed him." The challenge to the church is to learn how to receive Lazarus with love and in the name of Jesus, and how to be used of God to feed him. There is hope for Lazarus; and there is hope for the Church.

Conclusion

At one level this book is about honoring my brother, and recognizing his legacy. At a higher level it is about honoring the Lord Jesus Christ, and recognizing the work of the Holy Spirit. The underlying motivation has remained the idea that by sharing these stories and expressions of faith readers will be encouraged and motivated to a greater commitment of service. The ultimate goal is to bring the Word to someone whose life will be change by coming to know Him. In my efforts to compile and edit, I have come to know my brother better than I had known him before. He was truly a remarkable man whose life was packed full of the wonderful works of the Holy Spirit. Through the words that I have read over and over, I have come closer to the Lord; and I have experienced the wonderful work of the Holy Spirit in a remarkable new way. I have repeatedly been moved to shed tears and to whisper a prayer. I pray that readers will be touched and moved as well.